365 daily DEVOTIONS for BOYS

B&H KIDS
Nashville, Tennessee

978-1-4336-8822-5

Published by B&H Publishing Group,
Nashville, Tennessee

Dewey Decimal Classification: C242.2
Subject Heading: DEVOTIONAL LITERATURE / BOYS / CHRISTIAN LIFE

All Scripture quotations are taken from the Holman Christian Standard
Bible®, Copyright © 1999, 2000, 2002, 2003, 2009
by Holman Bible Publishers.

2 3 4 5 6 7 • 19 18 17 16 15

OUT WITH THE OLD

Your eyes saw me when I was formless;
all my days were written in Your book
and planned before a single one of
them began. —Psalm 139:16

Today begins a new year. By now you probably have a new calendar hanging on the wall or a new day planner with nothing yet written in it.

Want to know something cool? Before you were even born, God already had your calendar hanging on His wall with every day of your life written on it!

INCREDIBLY AWESOME

I will praise You because I have been remarkably and wonderfully made. Your works are wonderful, and I know this very well. —Psalm 139:14

You probably enjoy making things with your own hands. You consider your creation a masterpiece and proudly display it for others to see.

God felt the same way when He made you. You are an incredible creation that God is extremely proud of. You are His masterpiece! Have you thanked Him today?

MAKING CHANGES

Your hands made me and formed me; give me understanding so that I can learn Your commands. —Psalm 119:73

Did you make a New Year's resolution this year? If you did, you are not alone. If you really want to change something, why not consider asking God to help you understand what He wants you to do? Commit to learning and putting God's commands into practice. They will last longer than any resolution you could ever make!

PLANNED PURPOSE

I chose you before I formed you in the womb; I set you apart before you were born. I appointed you a prophet to the nations. —Jeremiah 1:5

Hide-and-seek is one of the best games of all time. Trying to find people who are hiding can be tons of fun. But what about finding your reason for being here—your purpose in life? God doesn't hide His plans for your life. Remember that God chose you and gave you a purpose before you were ever born. How awesome is that?

WHO'S ON DUTY?

You clothed me with skin and flesh, and wove me together with bones and tendons. You gave me life and faithful love, and Your care has guarded my life. —Job 10:11–12

Have you ever seen a lifeguard in action? If someone is in trouble, he does not hesitate to jump into action and save a swimmer from harm. When people sign up to be lifeguards, they know that caring for others is their job.

Did you know that God is your lifeguard? He offers constant care, love, and protection.

APPLE OF HIS EYE

Protect me as the pupil of Your eye;
hide me in the shadow of Your wings.
—Psalm 17:8

Has your mom ever told you that you are the apple of her eye? It's kind of a weird thing to tell somebody, but this phrase means that you are incredibly special and cherished to someone.

Many people give credit to King Alfred of Wessex for first using the phrase in AD 885, but David used it in the Bible before King Alfred was ever born. Remember today that you really are the apple of God's eye.

MY BFF

I have been with you wherever you have gone, and I have destroyed all your enemies before you. I will make a name for you like that of the greatest in the land. —2 Samuel 7:9

When someone tells you that you are his BFF, what do you think of? BFF means "best friends forever." A best friend is one who is there no matter what, someone who will always have your best interest in mind, and someone who will stand up and fight for you. You may have some great friends, but nobody will be a BFF like God. Let Him be your BFF today.

SMALL IS BIG

For by the grace given to me, I tell
everyone among you not to think of
himself more highly than he should think.
Instead, think sensibly, as God
has distributed a measure of faith
to each one. —Romans 12:3

Do you know someone who is a big shot at your school? Everyone knows people who think they are better than everyone else. God says that you should not think you are better than everyone else but you should show humility instead. A humble person will show others that they are more important than he is. Give it a try today with every person and in every situation.

A FRESH START

The merciful are blessed, for they will be shown mercy. —Matthew 5:7

Your friend has you in a headlock; you yell "Mercy!" and he lets you go. Sound familiar? There are many situations in which people say "Mercy!" and are given a chance to start over. It's no different with God. He gives you mercy each day and expects you to show mercy to others as well. How will you show mercy to others today?

LOVE OTHERS

Dear friends, let us love one another, because love is from God, and everyone who loves has been born of God and knows God. —1 John 4:7

Look around you. How many times do you hear people saying "I love you" to each other? People toss that phrase around like scrambled eggs in a pan, but why are people supposed to love one another?

God said that if you are in a relationship with Him, you are to love others. Tell those you care about today that you love them!

JANUARY 11

GOT A FRIEND?

A friend loves at all times, and a brother
is born for a difficult time.
—Proverbs 17:17

You may have developed a deep love for your electronics and gadgets. But do you have the same amount of love for friends?

It's much easier to say, "I love my music," than it is to spend time developing and investing love in your friends. Today, spend some time working on loving your friends more than your stuff because your friendships will last forever.

IN GOOD COMPANY

Do not be deceived: "Bad company corrupts good morals."
—1 Corinthians 15:33

Decisions, decisions, decisions! Every day you face choices and each decision seems to be more important than the previous. Out of all the decisions you will make in life, choosing your friends wisely ranks near the top. Every choice you make will have consequences—good or bad. So choose wisely today!

FOLLOW THE LEADER

Do not imitate what is evil,
but what is good. The one who does
good is of God; the one who does
evil has not seen God. —3 John 11

Have you ever played follow-the-leader? Whatever the leader did, you had to imitate him or risk being eliminated from the game. That may be OK when you are playing the game, but in life you must be careful when you follow other people and imitate what they do. To avoid costly mistakes, the only leader you should imitate is God. Give that a try today!

STOP THE BULLYING!

I am weary from my groaning; with my tears I dampen my pillow and drench my bed every night. My eyes are swollen from grief; they grow old because of all my enemies. Depart from me, all evildoers, for the LORD has heard the sound of my weeping. —Psalm 6:6–8

Being pushed around by others is not fun at all! Sometimes it seems like there is a bully waiting around every corner whose only purpose in life is to make your life miserable. God sees and knows about the bullies in your life. God's Word to you is not to fear them but to pray for them and ask Him to remove them. Who do you need to begin to pray for today?

DO WHAT?

You have heard that it was said,
Love your neighbor and hate your enemy.
But I tell you, love your enemies and
pray for those who persecute you.
—Matthew 5:43–44

Think of someone at school you just can't stand. Did more than one person come to mind? The world will tell you that it's OK to hate someone, but God doesn't think so. He wants you to love even those people you cannot stand. Today, pray and ask God to help you love that person. Who knows, he might just be a good friend in the making!

WHO'S AFRAID?

Be strong and courageous, all you who put your hope in the LORD. —Psalm 31:24

Dylan was afraid of the dark and his buddies knew it. On campouts they would play cruel tricks on him. One evening, just before dark, Dylan asked God to take away his fear of the darkness. Suddenly he felt good and strong inside. From that night on, he was not afraid anymore. He knew that God had answered his prayer.

LIKE A BIG BROTHER

He is the shield that protects you, the sword you boast in. Your enemies will cringe before you, and you will tread on their backs. —Deuteronomy 33:29

The neighborhood bully liked to threaten the younger guys. But little Kevin had a big brother who waited in the shadows one day. When Kevin kept walking toward the bully, he growled and drew back to punch Kevin. About that time, his big brother stepped from behind a tree. The war was over. God, like a big brother, protects you from the evil one.

SHARING THE VICTORY

For the LORD your God is the One who goes with you to fight for you against your enemies to give you victory.
—Deuteronomy 20:4

Your buddies seemed determined to do something wrong that would hurt someone. You tried to stop it, but they laughed at you and ignored you. You felt alone and left out. You knew you were right, and you prayed for God's help. Before anything happened, one of the guys decided to stand with you. You had won because God was with you.

WHO'S LISTENING IN?

A man with many friends may be harmed, but there is a friend who stays closer than a brother. —Proverbs 18:24

Going online is a lot of fun, and texting your friends is a great way to keep in touch. Before you know it, you can be connected to many friends, even to "friends of friends," whom you do not know very well. Some friends you can always count on, but some will let you down. Christ is a friend who will never disappoint you.

JUST A TEXT AWAY

I called to the LORD, who is worthy of
praise, and I was saved from my enemies.
—2 Samuel 22:4

Jason was in his bedroom texting his friend next door. Suddenly he heard loud noises downstairs, and a strange voice threatening his parents. He quickly called 911 and texted his friend, whose parents alerted another neighbor. When the robber heard the commotion outside, he ran away. Concerned friends were ready to help. God is instantly on call when you need Him.

JANUARY 21

ON STANDBY

Be strong and courageous; don't be terrified or afraid of them. For it is the LORD your God who goes with you; He will not leave you or forsake you.
—Deuteronomy 31:6

Nick was home from the hospital. For several nights his mother had sat by his bed. Nick's father felt that Nick no longer needed someone with him. He could call for help. Nick was afraid and called out in the night. His father answered. He had been in the room all night. Afraid? God, your heavenly Father, is always on standby for His children.

A DIFFERENT FEAR

Fear the LORD your God, and He will deliver you from the hand of all your enemies. —2 Kings 17:39

The word *fear* usually means "to be afraid of something or someone." That kind of fear makes people uncomfortable and unsure of what to do or think. To fear God, however, does not mean to be afraid of Him, but to respect Him. He is an all-powerful, awesome God who is anxious to do for you what you cannot do for yourself.

A READY GUIDE

Think about Him in all your ways, and
He will guide you on the right paths.
—Proverbs 3:6

When Jeremy's grandfather died, Jeremy was sad for many reasons. He missed the summer vacations at his grandparents' farm and all the fun things he and his grandfather did together. When Jeremy was growing up, he shared his problems with his grandfather.

Jeremy began reading the Bible every day and discovered that God is always available to guide him.

CHOICES! CHOICES!

I will honor those who honor Me, but those who despise Me will be disgraced.
—1 Samuel 2:30

How many choices do you make every day? Some are unimportant. Others will make a difference. Will I choose Jay or Peyton as a partner for my science project? Jay is more fun, but I will waste less time with Peyton. Serious choices deal with what is right or wrong. Wrong choices dishonor God.

TO STAND ALONE

Be alert, stand firm in the faith, act like a man, be strong. —1 Corinthians 16:13

It can be really lonely when you take a stand for what you know is right. Your best friends do something questionable. Do you give in and go with the crowd, or do you stand firm for what is right? Sometimes God helps you grow stronger in your faith during your "standing alone" times.

TO BE A MAN

My eager expectation and hope
is that I will not be ashamed about
anything, but that now as always, with
all boldness, Christ will be highly honored
in my body, whether by life or by death.
—Philippians 1:20

"We're looking for a few good men!" That is the call of one branch of the U.S. armed forces. What does it take to be a "good man"? What about one who tells the truth, doesn't run from difficulties, and believes in fair play?

The apostle Paul wanted to be strong and courageous for Christ. How important is it to you to "be a man" for Christ?

JANUARY 27

MY CHECKLIST

Finally brothers, whatever is true,
whatever is honorable, whatever is just,
whatever is pure, whatever is lovely,
whatever is commendable—if there is
any moral excellence and if there is
any praise—dwell on these things.
—Philippians 4:8

What do you think about? Are you constantly thinking of a new strategy for conquering the next level of your favorite video game? Are you trying to figure out a way to get your big brother back for being mean to you?

The Bible says that your thoughts should be focused on positive things that are pure in motive and commendable. Revenge is neither lovely nor excellent!

HEADS UP!

Be on your guard and diligently watch yourselves, so that you don't forget the things your eyes have seen and so that they don't slip from your mind as long as you live. —Deuteronomy 4:9

As he stormed into his room, Devin yelled at his mom, "You never get me anything!" Devin wanted a new video game, but his mother had not bought it for him.

Devin forgot that just last week his mom had bought him a new pair of shoes and a new Ripstik.

Today's verse reminds you to remember the good things that God has done for you and to not forget them!

DESPERATE PLUNGE

No one has greater love than this, that someone would lay down his life for his friends. —John 15:13

Ethan and I had been best friends since fourth grade. One summer we were fishing and our boat hit a stump and overturned. Ethan was caught underwater. I made a desperate plunge and jerked him loose. Fishermen nearby came to help. "Why did you do it?" Ethan asked me. "You're my best friend, and you nearly drowned!" Jesus didn't risk His life, He gave His life—for you!

THE ONLY WAY

Believe on the Lord Jesus, and you will be saved. —Acts 16:31

Take a minute to list a few things you believe in:

_____

_____

_____

_____

What made your list? There are probably many things that could be on your list, but the most important is Jesus. If you believe in Jesus and ask Him to be your Savior, the Bible says you will be a Christian.

BREAKING NEWS!

The following night, the Lord stood by him and said, "Have courage! For as you have testified about Me in Jerusalem, so you must also testify in Rome."
—Acts 23:11

When I was growing up, the only "breaking news" we got was when the paper boy rode down our street on his bike, waving a newspaper and shouting, "Extra! Extra! Read all about it!" Something unusual had happened, and we rushed out to buy a paper.

God wants you to share the good news that He gave His Son to save people from sin. Who will you tell?

A BOSS WHO'S NOT BOSSY

Then Jesus came near and said to them, "All authority has been given to Me in heaven and on earth." —Matthew 28:18

Sometimes guys struggle with authority. They don't want someone else telling them what to do, but you have to live under someone's authority. You will always have a boss. Reread today's verse. Jesus is the Master—or Lord—of everyone and everything, and He loves you. He wants what's best for you!

WHAT'S YOUR TREASURE?

For where your treasure is, there your heart will be also. —Matthew 6:21

What do you value most in the world? That's your treasure. Your treasure could be money, a sport, a trophy, a game system, a person, or Jesus. Whatever you value most will get your attention and time, and it will get your heart. You will love it more than anything else, but is it something that will last? A relationship with Jesus will last—forever!

WHATEVER

Whether you eat or drink, or whatever
you do, do everything for God's glory.
—1 Corinthians 10:31

Playing basketball, eating dinner, drinking a sports drink, reading a book, going to church . . . Whatever you do in your day wherever you are, God says to do it to honor Him. If you can't do something in good conscience to honor God, then you need to reconsider doing that thing—whatever it is.

ARE YOU SURE ABOUT THAT?

They were astonished at His teaching because His message had authority.
—Luke 4:32

Have you ever heard someone speak and wondered if he really knew what he was talking about? Jesus is totally not like that! Jesus is the Son of God. When He lived on the earth, people noticed that He was different. When He talked, people listened. He really knew what He was speaking about. He spoke with authority. He spoke with power.

DEVIL-DEFEATING, BIG TIME BOSS

Now that He has gone into heaven,
He is at God's right hand with angels,
authorities, and powers subjected
to Him. —1 Peter 3:22

Jesus lived without sin and died on the cross for your sins. Then on the third day, He came back to life in His body and defeated the devil. Later, He went back to heaven to take the seat of power next to the Father and He now rules over all powers in heaven and on the earth. He really is Boss, whether you accept it or not!

HOW BELIEVABLE ARE YOU?

Speak truth to one another.
—Zechariah 8:16

You've probably heard the story of the boy who cried wolf. Do you know anyone like that? My younger brother used to tell lies all the time. He told my mom he loaded the dishwasher when I had loaded it. He promised he finished his homework even though he hadn't even started. Pretty soon, no one in my family believed a word my brother said. It took my brother years to earn back our trust. The Bible says God wants you to speak the truth. How honest are you?

DISTRACTED

Let your eyes look forward; fix your
gaze straight ahead. —Proverbs 4:25

Ever been distracted? Drivers can be distracted when
they are eating, texting, talking, or reading. It's dangerous! The same is true for Christians. Instead of focusing on
Jesus, you might get distracted by a sport, a hobby, or even
a girl. Instead of looking straight ahead to Jesus, you're
distracted by side things. Fix your eyes on Him today.

WILL YOU PASS THE TEST?

A man who endures trials is blessed, because when he passes the test he will receive the crown of life that God has promised to those who love Him.
—James 1:12

Perseverance is sticking it out. Your team is down by 30 points, but you play hard until the end.

You've been working on math for an hour and are only halfway finished, but you stick it out until you've completed it. That's perseverance.

You are being pressured by a friend to do something with which you disagree, but you stay true to your beliefs. That's perseverance.

A GENTLE NUDGE

I always do my best to have a clear
conscience toward God and men.
—Acts 24:16

Ever had that gentle nudge inside that what you were about to do was not right? Having a clear conscience means you don't ignore that gentle nudge inside—your conscience. Having a clear conscience brings peace to your life. An unclear conscience brings guilt, shame, and unrest. When you feel that gentle nudge, pay attention!

SET FREE TO REALLY LIVE

Speak and act as those who will be judged by the law of freedom. —James 2:12

People who have surrendered their lives to Jesus as Lord and Savior have been set free, but they haven't been set free to live as they please. If you're a Christian, you've been freed from sin and are now free to live for Christ. Let your words and actions show that Jesus is in control.

ANGER ARROWS

Be angry and do not sin.
—Ephesians 4:26

Sometimes your anger can get the best of you. Anger is not always wrong, but it is dangerous when people take out their anger on innocent people. Your brother or sister, your mom or dad, and your friends at school can become the target for your angry arrows. Try dropping your arrows instead of firing them.

BREAK OUT THE CUFFS

We demolish arguments and every
high-minded thing that is raised up
against the knowledge of God, taking
every thought captive to obey Christ.
—2 Corinthians 10:4-5

Jesus is the devil-defeating, big time Boss of the world. He rules over everything. If you are His follower, watch out for thoughts or beliefs that don't demonstrate that Jesus is Lord. The next time you want to make fun of a friend, talk back to your parents, or disobey a coach, handcuff those thoughts and hand them over to Jesus.

THAT'S NOT FAIR!

God is not unjust; He will not forget your work. —Hebrews 6:10

God is a fair God. In fact, He's more than fair. He's so far beyond fair that it's difficult to comprehend. Sin deserves punishment and that punishment is death. You sin, you pay. That's fair. Yet God sent His one and only Son to take your punishment for you. That's way beyond fair. God is not unjust. He is good, and He loves you.

SUFFERING SUPPORT

The God of all grace . . . will personally
restore, establish, strengthen, and support
you after you have suffered a little.
—1 Peter 5:10

Sometimes bad times come. Sometimes you suffer because of your faith in Christ. You may be laughed at for your Christian beliefs, but God doesn't laugh. He supports you.

Sometimes you have to suffer for your faith in Jesus, but it's only for a little while. Through it all, God personally supports, strengthens, and carries you. You can count on Him.

I'LL STAND WITH YOU

Each one helps the other, and says to another, "Take courage!" —Isaiah 41:6

Michael's coach announced that the baseball games would be on Sundays. None of the other boys seemed to care, but Michael wasn't going to give up church every week to be on the team, no matter how much he wanted to play! Brian agreed with Michael but he was afraid to speak up. Finally, he talked to Michael and said, "You're right. I'll stand with you."

LIGHT IT UP

All these were approved through their faith, but they did not receive what was promised, since God had provided something better for us, so that they would not be made perfect without us.
—Hebrews 11:39–40

Has the electricity ever gone out in your house? Weren't you glad when your father turned on the flashlight so you could see him?

The heroes in the Old Testament trusted God even when they couldn't see Him. Jesus is the light that reveals the heavenly Father, even in complete darkness.

A FAMILY PORTRAIT

Let us cleanse ourselves from every
impurity of the flesh and spirit,
completing our sanctification complete
in the fear of God. —2 Corinthians 7:1

Do people say you are strong like your dad or caring like your mom? You've received many traits from your parents.

The Bible describes Christians as being sons of God. He is your heavenly Father, so you should be like Him. You love because He loves. You try to be fair because He is just. You forgive others because He forgives you. Get the picture?

YOU GROW WHAT YOU SOW

A gentle answer turns away anger,
but a harsh word stirs up wrath.
—Proverbs 15:1

When you plant corn seeds, do you expect to grow turnips? Do you plant green beans to grow carrots? Of course not!

But how often do you yell back at someone who yells at you? Or if someone hits you, do you hit him back? The Bible says that planting seeds of love is the way to grow kindness from the other person. What will you grow?

TRUST IS A MUST

These all died in faith without having received the promises, but they saw them from a distance, greeted them, and confessed that they were foreigners and temporary residents on the earth.
—Hebrews 11:13

You probably look forward to birthdays because you know there will be presents, even if you don't know exactly what they will be.

The Bible tells about men who trusted God even when they couldn't see exactly what God promised them. Trust God even when you don't know exactly what He's doing.

THE YOKE'S ON YOU

Take up My yoke and learn from Me.
—Matthew 11:29

Do you feel relieved when an extremely difficult test is over?

The Old Testament reminds people that they are not prepared to pass God's test. In the New Testament, the Bible says that Jesus has already taken the test for you! All you have to do is believe He did it, and you'll get an A.

SURF'S UP, DUDE!

For I do not understand what I am doing, because I do not practice what I want to do, but I do what I hate. —Romans 7:15

"Ah! Come on!" Nick said when his surfer crashed into an iceberg on Club Penguin™. No matter how hard he tried to beat that game, he couldn't keep from making mistakes.

Trying to live like Jesus is in some ways similar to playing a computer game. You mess up sometimes, no matter how hard you try not to. What's important is that you keep trying.

DANGEROUS DISCIPLESHIP

Christ also suffered for you, leaving you an example, so that you should follow in His steps. —1 Peter 2:21

If your friend told you to jump off a bridge, would you do it? No! That would be harmful and foolish.

Following Jesus actually does mean taking risks. Many missionaries, pastors, and other Christian leaders are serving in dangerous places. Will you obey Jesus, even if it is dangerous?

READ MY LIPS!

How can a young man keep his
way pure? By keeping Your word.
—Psalm 119:9

How do you know you're supposed to keep your room clean, take out the trash, or pick up after yourself? You know because your parents told you to do it.

God tells His children what they need to do too. He uses words to tell you, and those words are written in the Bible.

LASTING LOVE

Now these three remain: faith, hope, and love. But the greatest of these is love.
—1 Corinthians 13:13

Love is great because its value lasts forever. Think about faith and hope. In heaven you will no longer need faith and hope because you'll be with Jesus. You won't need faith when you see Him face-to-face, and what you've hoped for has finally happened. Love, however, is eternal. Its usefulness never ends.

FEBRUARY 25

SEEK AND FIND

I sought the LORD, and He answered me
and delivered me from all my fears.
—Psalm 34:4

Sometimes it's not good to be alone. Walking at night, facing the class bully, and riding your bike past a mean dog are just a few scary situations in which you might want someone to be with you.

Did you know that God is everywhere all the time? When you are afraid, ask Him to help. Pray and trust that He is taking care of you.

DO YOU HEAR ME?

There He revealed Himself to Samuel by His word. —1 Samuel 3:21

Another name for the Bible is God's Word. The Bible contains all the words God chose to record for people. Through the Bible you can discover great things about God, yourself, and how Jesus restores your relationship with God.

If you want to know God, spend time reading His Word!

LOVING THE UNLOVABLE

Love your enemies, do what is good to those who hate you. —Luke 6:27

"Forgive him. He doesn't know any better." Do you say that when someone laughs at you? Is that your response when a bully pushes you?

That's what Jesus said as He was dying on the cross. He gave His life to pay for the sins of people who hated Him. They were His enemies, but He still loved them and did what was best for them.

A LAW OF LOVE

Love does no wrong to a neighbor. Love, therefore, is the fulfillment of the law. —Romans 13:10

Did you know that the Ten Commandments can be summarized by two statements? Love God. Love others. According to Jesus in Matthew 22:37–40, obeying the Commandments is that simple.

Check it out for yourself by reading the Commandments in Exodus 20. The first four tell you how to love God. And the last six Commandments tell you how to love other people.

EXPOSED

My Lord, if I have indeed found favor in
Your sight, my Lord, please go with us.
Even though this is a stiff-necked people,
forgive our wrongdoing and sin, and
accept us as Your own possession.
—Exodus 34:9

Have you ever wondered why some mirrors are surrounded by bright lights? The lights are there to help people see their flaws. The mirror in your bathroom may help you see dirt on your face or food in your teeth. God's Word does a similar thing for His people. The Bible shines a bright light on your wrongdoing and sin so you can know how to change.

RUNWAY LIGHTS

Pay careful attention, then, to how you walk—not as unwise people but as wise.
—Ephesians 5:15

Pilots are very careful when they take off and land—especially at night! No matter how long they've been pilots, they still pay careful attention to their runway lights so they don't crash. In a similar way, God wants you to pay careful attention to every decision you make, even if you've been a Christian for a long time.

IN THE SPOTLIGHT

But honor the Messiah as Lord in your hearts. Always be ready to give a defense to anyone who asks you for a reason for the hope that is in you. However, do this with gentleness and respect, keeping your conscience clear, so that when you are accused, those who denounce your Christian life will be put to shame.
—1 Peter 3:15–16

When spotlights are put on people during performances, the entire crowd watches them to see what they'll do. Some people thrive in the spotlight. Some get very nervous when they know all eyes are on them. If anyone ever asks why you believe in Jesus or why you have hope, the spotlight is on you! Will you be ready to answer?

PERMANENT LIGHT

Jesus spoke to them again: "I am the light of the world. Anyone who follows Me will never walk in the darkness but will have the light of life." —John 8:12

The earth receives its light from the sun, yet even though human beings depend so much on the sun's light to see during the day, every night the sunlight vanishes. Darkness returns.

Things are different spiritually though. Jesus says that if you follow Him, you will never walk in the darkness. He will be a permanent light to guide your way!

LET IT SHINE!

No one lights a lamp and puts in under a basket, but rather on a lampstand, and it gives light for all who are in the house. In the same way, let your light shine before men, so that they may see your good works and give glory to your Father in heaven. —Matthew 5:15-16

Wouldn't it be pointless to turn on a lamp and then cover it up? Its light would be useless!

Jesus said that God has made you like a light, and He wants you to shine. God wants other people to see how He shines through you. Never try to hide your faith in Jesus or cover up what He's doing. Shine brightly and proudly!

LIGHT FOR EVERYONE

Then everyone who calls on the name of the Lord will be saved. —Acts 2:21

Sometimes people are tempted to believe that salvation and forgiveness are only granted to those who live squeaky clean lives and who are super-godly. But God says otherwise! Everyone who turns from his sin and puts his faith in Jesus will receive salvation. That's great news! So today, make sure you are turning to Jesus for your salvation—not to your own good deeds.

A LIGHT THAT NEVER GOES OUT

I have written these things to you who believe in the name of the Son of God, so that you may know that you have eternal life. —1 John 5:13

Light bulbs always burn out. Newer energy-efficient bulbs may last a long time, but they eventually will need to be replaced too. There is nothing in this life that is permanent. Everything is temporary. In today's verse, John tells Christians that they can have absolute confidence in something that will last forever: the eternal life they will share with Jesus!

NO HAZARD LIGHTS

I am sure of this, that He who started a good work in you will carry it on to completion until the day of Christ Jesus.
—Philippians 1:6

Have you ever seen a stranded car with its lights flashing? Those are hazard lights. They warn other drivers that the car has broken down and can go no further.

When it comes to spiritual growth, Christians can have confidence they'll never break down like that. They might slow down or have problems, but God will keep them running. No need for hazard lights!

NIGHT LIGHT

For I am persuaded that not even death or life, angels or rulers, things present or things to come, hostile powers, height or depth, or any other created thing will have the power to separate us from the love of God that is in Christ Jesus our Lord! —Romans 8:38-39

Even adults use night lights sometimes. That little light can calm people and convince them that all will be well in the darkness of the night. What Paul is telling readers in this verse is that even when dark times come and you suffer through terrible things, you can have confidence that God still loves you. That will never change—even in life's hardest times!

THE LIGHTHOUSE

But I am not ashamed, because I know the One I believed in and am persuaded that He is able to guard what has been entrusted to me until that day.
—2 Timothy 1:12

When ships approach the shore at night, their captains look for lighthouses to guide them and guard them against any danger of crashing into the rocks. Captains do everything possible to protect their cargo. Likewise, God protects the good news of Jesus from any danger. Even when His messengers are threatened or mistreated, He guards and protects the Good News so it can keep being spread worldwide!

GOD'S GREEN LIGHT

Let us draw near with a true heart
in full assurance of faith, our hearts
sprinkled clean from an evil conscience
and our bodies washed in pure water.
—Hebrews 10:22

You might have a hard time imagining that God could let you be close to Him. You might think, I've disobeyed Him so much! You might think there's a red light, telling you to stop and stay away. But if you trust in Jesus' death and resurrection, you have been cleaned and washed. You're forgiven and have a green light to draw near!

MARCH 12

LIVING IN THE LIGHT

We know that everyone who has been born of God does not sin, but the One who is born of God keeps him, and the evil one does not touch him.
—1 John 5:18

Imagine spending several years in a dark cave and then coming out into daylight. Your eyes might hurt at first, but you'd be foolish to go back to the cave's darkness!

Spiritually speaking, Christians shouldn't choose to return to the darkness of sin. Instead, if you've been born of God, you should live in obedience to Him. Today, avoid sinning and live in the light!

HEAVENLY LIGHT

After Jesus was baptized, He went
up immediately from the water.
—Matthew 3:16

Most people have heard the phrase, "Do as I say, but not as I do." Sometimes authority figures demand things of others but refuse to do them themselves. Jesus wasn't like that. He wanted others to be baptized, so He was willing to be baptized too. Jesus set an example and God looked on Jesus' baptism with great approval!

MARCH 14

DELIGHT

There came a voice from heaven: This is
My beloved Son. I take delight in Him!
—Matthew 3:17

God the Father took delight in Jesus. Why? He delighted in Jesus because everything He did—being baptized, resisting temptation, healing, preaching, and being crucified for sinners—was done out of love for the Father.

Today, if you are united with Jesus, when God looks at you, He sees the perfection of Jesus. That means God takes delight in you too!

THE LIGHT REVEALED

John testified, "I watched the Spirit descending from heaven like a dove, and He rested on Him. I didn't know Him, but He who sent me to baptize with water told me, 'The One you see the Spirit descending and resting on—He is the One who baptizes with the Holy Spirit.' I have seen and testified that He is the Son of God!" —John 1:32–34

When Jesus first started preaching, people had serious doubts about who He claimed to be. But John the Baptist didn't. When he baptized Jesus, John saw the Holy Spirit descend from heaven and rest on Jesus! God made it perfectly clear that this really was His Son.

Has God convinced you of who Jesus really is? If so, share in John's excitement today!

CHILDREN OF THE LIGHT

The Spirit Himself testifies together with our spirit that we are God's children. —Romans 8:16

Do you have a friend with whom you can talk about anything? That is how the Holy Spirit wants to be with you.

He has some important things to tell you. One of the most special things He wants to tell you is that you are a child of God! No matter what happens in life, your heavenly Father will be with you!

MARCH 17

FREEDOM!

Therefore, no condemnation now exists for those in Christ Jesus, because the Spirit's law of life in Christ Jesus has set you free from the law of sin and of death. —Romans 8:1-2

If you have admitted your sin, believed in Jesus, and confessed Him as Lord and Savior, then God sees you as His child. When He looks at you, He doesn't see your sin.

God takes your sin seriously, but He has forgiven you. Sin is not your master! God freed you from sin and death!

A LIGHT FOR YOUR PATH

Therefore, we were buried with Him by baptism into death, in order that, just as Christ was raised from the dead by the glory of the Father, so we too may walk in a new way of life. —Romans 6:4

Have you ever been playing a board game and really wished you could redo your turn? Maybe you were going to lose or you didn't do your best.

Salvation through Jesus is a completely new turn! You have a brand new life. All the old mistakes you made are gone and a new life has begun!

A LIGHT BULB GOES ON!

As they were traveling down the road, they came to some water. The eunuch said, "Look, there's water! What would keep me from being baptized?"
And Philip said, "If you believe with all your heart you may." And he replied, "I believe that Jesus Christ is the Son of God." —Acts 8:36-37

If this light bulb has never gone on in your life, today can be your day. The eunuch heard the truth about Jesus. He decided to put his faith in Jesus.

If you are ready to admit, believe, and confess your faith in Jesus just like this man did, take to your parent or pastor. Then be baptized to start your new life with Jesus!

NOT A LIGHT MEAL

This is My body, which is given for you.
Do this in remembrance of Me.
—Luke 22:19

This was the first Lord's Supper. When you eat the bread and drink the juice, remember the sacrifice Jesus made for your salvation.

The bread and juice are powerful symbols of Jesus' death on the cross. One more thing to remember is that Jesus is no longer dead; He defeated death and is alive!

REMEMBERING THE LIGHT

This cup is the new covenant established in My blood. Do this, as often as you drink it, in remembrance of Me.
—1 Corinthians 11:25

When Jesus gave His life, a new promise, or covenant, from God was put into place.

The sacrifices of the Old Testament didn't need to be made anymore. Jesus had sacrificed once for all. It made a whole new way for people who follow Jesus.

Jesus shed His own blood to start a new way for those who believe. That is worth remembering!

EXAM ROOM LIGHTS

A man should examine himself; in this way he should eat the bread and drink of the cup. —1 Corinthians 11:28

Before taking the Lord's Supper God reminds you to look into your own heart and life.

It is like getting a flashlight to look around your home for something you've lost. What you're looking for in your heart is anything that would not please God like meanness, pride, unforgiveness, or disrespect. Ask God to make your heart pure before you take the Lord's Supper.

RECEIVING THE LIGHT

"Repent," Peter said to them, "and be baptized, each of you, in the name of Jesus Christ for the forgiveness of your sins, and you will receive the gift of the Holy Spirit." —Acts 2:38

When you decide to follow Jesus something very special happens: the Holy Spirit comes and lives in your heart.

The Holy Spirit lives in people who have trusted Jesus as their Savior. He comforts you when you are hurting and reminds you of the right things to do. The Holy Spirit is a great gift.

BRIGHTER LIGHT

Seek to excel in building up the church.
—1 Corinthians 14:12

You have things that you do well. What is your best thing?

Whatever you do best can be used by God to make the church better and stronger. Think of ways you can use what you do well to honor God. In the next week find a way to do at least one of those things.

A NEW WAY

I have baptized you with water, but He
will baptize you with the Holy Spirit.
—Mark 1:8

John the Baptist had been baptizing people before
Jesus began preaching and teaching. John let everyone
know that what Jesus did was different and better than
anything else.

Think about how far a baby can throw a baseball compared to a professional baseball player. There's no com-
parison, right? That is what John the Baptist was saying
about the things he was doing compared to Jesus.

SPEED OF LIGHT

Why delay? Get up and be baptized, and wash away your sins by calling on His name. —Acts 22:16

Putting things off is easy, but it's usually a bad idea. Waiting to put your life in God's hand is one of the worst ideas ever.

If you know someone who is putting off calling out to Jesus for salvation, read him this verse this weekend. There is no good excuse for delay!

POWER FOR YOUR LIGHT

But you will receive power when the Holy Spirit has come on you, and you will be My witnesses in Jerusalem, in all Judea and Samaria, and the ends of the earth. —Acts 1:8

God does not just save you and then send you on your way to live the rest of your life on your own. He gives you power to live a great life.

The Holy Spirit reminds you to make right choices. He also gives you the ability to make those good choices. Living life like this is a bright light to everyone around you!

MARCH 28

ULTIMATE POWER SOURCE

Our gospel did not come to you in word
only, but also in power, in the Holy
Spirit, and with much assurance.
—1 Thessalonians 1:5

God's Good News is powerful. Guys love powerful things: muscles, horsepower, strength. Guys like power!

The power of God is ultimate. His Good News is the most powerful act of all time: through His death and resurrection, Jesus beat sin and death! What seemed weak—dying on the cross—was actually part of God's powerful plan.

IS THE LIGHT ON?

This is His command: that we believe
in the name of His Son Jesus Christ, and
love one another as He commanded us.
—1 John 3:23

Have you ever stumbled through a dark room? Most of the time the first thing you do is turn on the light!

Salvation is not the end of God's plan for your life. It is like turning the light on—the first step in your journey with Him. After the light is on you can live the rest of life the way God planned for you.

WHERE DID THAT COME FROM?

For you are saved by grace you are saved through faith, and this is not from yourselves; it is God's gift—not from works, so that no one can boast.
—Ephesians 2:8–9

God's gift to you is salvation. There is nothing you can do to earn it. There is nothing you can do to lose it.

You may have been paid for doing something. Maybe you got a reward for doing something good. But you have probably also received a gift that was not a payment or a reward. This is like salvation—it is a gift!

SHINE YOUR LIGHT

Be doers of the word and not hearers only. —James 1:22

Think of the darkest place you have ever been. Did you have a flashlight? As soon as a light shines in the darkness the darkness disappears!

You are like God's flashlight. When you do good things (helping someone, being kind, praying for a friend), you are like a bright light. Doing good helps others see God's love.

FOLLOW THE LEADER

He said to them all, "If anyone wants to come with Me, he must deny himself, take up his cross daily, and follow Me."
—Luke 9:23

Following a leader—whether a teacher, coach, pastor, or even a teammate—requires putting your own interests second. Being a follower takes a special person, someone who doesn't mind working for a reward that many people wouldn't recognize or understand. Who do you follow? Follow Jesus!

SPEND TIME WITH HIM

Peter said to Jesus, "Lord, it's good for us to be here!" —Matthew 17:4

Peter knew that every minute spent listening to and learning from Jesus was a minute well spent. Is there someone you respect and whose counsel you cherish? Treasure the time you spend with that person. Try to see what makes him tick, what values shape the way he thinks or feels, and learn from him.

JESUS, GOD'S REFLECTION

He is the radiance of His glory, the
exact expression of His nature, and He
sustains all things by His powerful word.
—Hebrews 1:3

If you want to know what God is like, you can see Him in Jesus. Can you be a good reflection of Jesus on the earth so your friends will know something more about Him through your example? What characteristics would they talk about when describing you to other people? Would you recognize yourself? Let Jesus shine through you.

JESUS IN THE FLESH

The Word became flesh and took up
residence among us. —John 1:14

When Jesus became a man, He felt the same pain you do. He suffered the same sunburn, mosquito bites, sprained ankles, and jammed fingers. He is uniquely able to understand your life and to be your Savior. Did Jesus ever fail a test in school or miss an important free throw in a basketball game? Probably not, but He understands when you do.

APRIL 5

LIVING THE LIFE

I have come so that they may have life and have it in abundance. —John 10:10

One of Jesus' great promises is that your life can be joyful and eternal if you believe in Him. That's something to look forward to when your history test is difficult and you're having trouble with friends. You can feel a special joy in your life in any situation.

WATCHING THE SHEEP

I am the good shepherd. I know My own sheep, and they know Me. —John 10:14

If you've seen one sheep, you've seen them all: thick, curly wool, four legs, a tail, two eyes, and a nose. To you and me, they all look the same! But a shepherd knows the sheep as individuals, and they stay close to him for protection and food. Jesus, the Good Shepherd, knows you even better and provides for you in many of the same ways. Stick close to Him!

AT HOME WITH JESUS

Our citizenship is in heaven, from which we also eagerly wait for a Savior, the Lord Jesus Christ. —Philippians 3:20

You are a citizen of your hometown, your state, and the United States. More importantly, you have the promise that Jesus has an eternal home for you in heaven. If you are a Christian, your citizenship is in heaven. To someday be home with Jesus will be great!

THE GREATEST GIFT

This is how we have come to know love:
He laid down His life for us.
—1 John 3:16

Sacrificial living is putting the interests of others ahead of your own, and you should practice that regularly. The feelings of satisfaction you get from doing someone a favor or giving a gift are often very similar. Jesus made the ultimate sacrifice and paid the ultimate price by giving His life for you. That's the greatest gift!

THE GREATEST ONE

He is the blessed and only Sovereign, the
King of kings and the Lord of lords.
—1 Timothy 6:15

Timothy described Jesus perfectly. All people on the earth and the angels in heaven bow down and worship Him. He deserves your love, respect, and devotion. You are unworthy of the blessings He has given you, so praise and thank Him always.

WONDER OF WONDERS

You are great and perform wonders;
You alone are God. —Psalm 86:10

Sometimes people put too much emphasis on the deeds of earthly heroes. These heroes' successes are temporary. God's power is everlasting and nothing else can compare. How does a winning goal compare with calming the sea? Can stopping a penalty shot in soccer match up with healing the sick? God is great!

KEEP THE FAITH

"Daughter," He said to her, "your faith has made you well." —Mark 5:34

Faith is a giant step between what you see, feel, hear, and touch, and what you believe. Jesus wants you to take a step of faith and believe in Him as the Son of God. The woman who touched Jesus and was healed took a huge step of faith to approach the Savior. Will you?

HAVING HOPE

May the God of hope fill you with
all joy and peace as you believe
in Him so that you may overflow
with hope in the power of
the Holy Spirit. —Romans 15:13

Being joyful all the time is not easy. You might get a poor grade on a test. You and a friend might have a disagreement. But God promises that believing in Him can help you have a positive outlook all the time. Disappointments are temporary. God is always for you.

CALMING INFLUENCE

He got up and rebuked the wind and the raging waves. So they ceased, and there was a calm. —Luke 8:24

Jesus has power over God's entire creation. His power over nature saved the frightened disciples. Jesus can calm your fears about the problems you face every day in school, in your neighborhood, or at home. The only thing you have to do is ask Him for His help.

TAKE THE FIRST STEP

He saw Jesus, fell facedown,
and begged Him: "Lord, if You are
willing, You can make me clean."
—Luke 5:12

Jesus' promise of forgiveness never goes away. Will you take it or leave it? Whenever you call on Him, He can make your paths straight, but it is your responsibility to ask for forgiveness when you fall short. Like a baseball pitcher, he won't throw a strike before the catcher signals which kind of pitch to throw.

A REASON TO CHEER

When the crowds saw this, they were
awestruck and gave glory to God
who had given such authority to men.
—Matthew 9:8

Crowds at sporting events cheer for great touchdowns, three-point shots, home runs, goals, long putts—you name it. Imagine how loud it would be in a sold-out stadium if a crowd got to see Jesus heal the sick, walk on water, or calm the storms. Now that's a reason to cheer!

THE ULTIMATE MIRACLE

Go quickly and tell His disciples,
"He has been raised from the dead."
—Matthew 28:7

Jesus performed different kinds of miracles. He healed people's diseases. He calmed storms. He multiplied food. He walked on water. All of these miracles were to show that He was not just another person; He is God. His greatest miracle was His last one when He was raised from the dead. This is the best way you can know that Jesus is God!

KNOW WHO JESUS REALLY IS

Hosanna! Blessed is He who comes in the name of the Lord! —Mark 11:9

Large crowds shouted to Jesus as He arrived in Jerusalem during His triumphal entry. A few days later the crowds shouted, "Crucify Him!" Why the change? It's because they misunderstood who Jesus is. They thought He was a political leader when He is actually a spiritual Savior. Don't follow Jesus based on who you want Him to be; follow Him based on who He is.

GOD PROMISED IT

He promised long ago through His prophets in the Holy Scriptures. —Romans 1:2

Has someone ever broken a promise he made to you? It's difficult to trust people when they break promises. God has made plenty of promises in the Bible, such as His promise way back in the Old Testament to send Jesus. God keeps all of His promises. Isn't that wonderful? You can trust Him!

APRIL 19

PLANNED FROM THE BEGINNING

He was destined before the foundation of the world, but was revealed at the end of the times for you. —1 Peter 1:20

Before He created anything, God knew that people would rebel against Him and need forgiveness. God's plan to send Jesus to pay the sin penalty for people was in place before Adam and Eve ever ate the forbidden fruit. Nothing surprises God. Are you going through a difficult time? God knows and has a plan for that too!

A SAVIOR

God did not send His Son into the world that He might condemn the world, but that the world might be saved through Him. —John 3:17

Pointing out problems is easy. Offering solutions is a lot more difficult. God didn't send Jesus to the earth to point out problems; He sent Jesus to be the solution and to provide forgiveness for people.

How about you? Have you accepted Jesus' solution for your sin? Are you sharing this solution with your friends? Who do you know that needs God's forgiveness?

HE CAME TO TEACH

When Jesus had finished this sermon, the crowds were astonished at His teaching.
—Matthew 7:28

Think about your favorite teachers. Why do you like them? They probably care about you and do a good job of helping you learn.

Jesus was an amazing teacher because He loved people and He explained God's truth to them in ways they could understand. The Bible can be challenging at times, but you have a great Teacher.

HE CAME TO SAVE

The Son of Man has come to seek and to save the lost. —Luke 19:10

Baseball players have one goal: winning games. Hitting home runs, striking out opposing batters, and even scoring runs are all important, but they are secondary to the main purpose of winning games.

When Jesus came to the earth He had one purpose as well: to save people. His miracles, teachings, and other activities were important, but they were not His main purpose. Jesus came to provide salvation.

TRUST HIS POWER

He demonstrated this power in the Messiah by raising Him from the dead and seating Him at His right hand in the heavens. —Ephesians 1:20

God's power is so strong that not even death could keep Jesus down. His power will help you through all of the storms of life. Jesus is with God now, in heaven, sitting right beside Him. God is watching over you and wants you to trust in His power, not your own.

CELEBRATE JESUS!

The Lord has certainly been raised!
—Luke 24:34

I enjoy going to party stores. They sell great items to make all kinds of celebrations fun. Everyone likes a party; the fact that there are stores selling items just for parties proves that!

Today you have the greatest reason to celebrate—the resurrection of Jesus! Treat today as one giant party celebrating Jesus who lives!

KNOW THE ONE

My goal is to know Him and the power of His resurrection. —Philippians 3:10

There's a huge difference between knowing of someone and knowing someone. I know of St. Louis Cardinals' first basemen Albert Pujols, but I don't know him because we've never met.

How about you and Jesus? Do you know of Jesus or do you know Him? Get to know Jesus as your friend; it's the best thing you will ever do.

HE BRINGS FREEDOM

Having been liberated from sin, you
became enslaved to righteousness.
—Romans 6:18

Imagine being forced to walk around for a day with a heavy cinder block strapped to your back. Now imagine doing that for a week, for a month, or for years. Now imagine what it would feel like if someone removed the block from your back. That is a picture of what Jesus does for you when you allow Him to take your sin from you. That's freedom!

APRIL 27

HE BRINGS PEACE

Let the peace of the Messiah, to which you were also called in one body, control your hearts. Be thankful. —Colossians 3:15

What do you worry about? Doing well in school? Making friends? Having enough money? Everyone worries about things; however, God doesn't want you to. He wants you to trust in Him and allow Him to give you His peace. When you remember that God is in control and that He cares about your concerns even more than you do, you will have peace.

BELIEVE IT!

If you confess with your mouth, "Jesus is Lord," and believe in your heart that God raised Him from the dead, you will be saved. —Romans 10:9

When the Bible talks about belief, it is talking about more than just knowing something; belief means trusting in something. You can know a chair will hold you up if you sit on it, but you don't really trust in the chair until you actually sit down. Knowing that Jesus is Lord and Savior is not enough—you have to trust Him with your life too.

SEE IT FOR YOURSELF

We have heard for ourselves and know that this really is the Savior of the world. —John 4:42

Most people give Thomas a hard time for wanting to see the resurrected Jesus. He's even known as "doubting Thomas"! Actually, you can learn something from Thomas. Faith in Jesus must be personal—it has to be yours. No one can trust in Jesus for you. No one can love Jesus for you. You wouldn't want them to anyway! Enjoy knowing Jesus personally.

THE ONLY WAY

Jesus told him, "I am the way, the truth, and the life. No one comes to the Father except through Me." —John 14:6

Examine a map and you will see many different ways to drive from Baltimore, Maryland, to Philadelphia, Pennsylvania, but only one way to drive from Key Largo, Florida, to Key West, Florida. The Bible, God's "map" for life, shows you there is only one way to reach God—through Jesus Christ. He is the only way.

PASS OR BE PASSED

Just as you want others to do for you, do the same for them. —Luke 6:31

Curt's favorite words in basketball were, "I'm open!" He always wanted the ball but never seemed to pass it. Pretty soon, everyone learned not to pass to Curt. Only when he learned to share the ball did Curt find people willing to pass to him. God wants you to treat others as you want to be treated.

THE SAFE ZONE

When she could no longer hide him, she got a papyrus basket for him and coated it with asphalt and pitch. She placed the child in it and set it among the reeds by the bank of the Nile. —Exodus 2:3

My favorite feeling is sliding into home plate during a baseball game and hearing the umpire shout, "Safe!" Did you know that God designed families to be a safe place for you when life feels out of control? Moses' mother did everything she could to keep him safe. When you need rest and protection, go to a place where you feel at home!

DISTANT RELATIONS

Then his sister stood at a distance in order to see what would happen to him.
—Exodus 2:4

My brothers are 10 and 15 years older than me, so we never grew close as kids. Still, I know that if I have trouble, I can call either one of them. Like Moses' sister, they might stand back at a distance, but they will always watch out for me. Whether your family is close or distant, you can still care for each other.

BABY FEVER

> When she opened it, she saw the child—a little boy, crying. She felt sorry for him and said, "This is one of the Hebrew boys." —Exodus 2:6

Ever see women with a newborn baby? They go absolutely crazy, holding the baby and cooing at her. If you're like most guys, you look and mutter, "Yeah, that's a baby." As silly as girls and women act around babies, be glad. Imagine what it would be like for babies if only men cared for them! God's plan is perfect. Praise Him for that.

YOU'RE ADOPTED

When the child grew older, she brought him to Pharaoh's daughter, and he became her son. —Exodus 2:10

My parents didn't adopt me. They've put up with me from day one. Likewise, I haven't adopted any kids. But there's something special about choosing to bring a child into your home. It's a special love, the kind of love God shows people. I'm adopted as a child of God. If you are a Christian, God chose you and brought you into His family. That's great love!

BRINGING SOMETHING BACK

She said, "He gave me these six measures of barley, because he said, 'Don't go back to your mother-in-law empty-handed.'"
—Ruth 3:17

I have a flock of chickens that lay about two dozen eggs each day. I sell eggs to pay for chicken feed, but I really enjoy giving eggs to my mother, brothers, and church family. Why do I enjoy feeding the freeloaders? Easy—they're my family! They share with me. I share with them. That's what God wants.

THE CARETAKER

Naomi took the child, placed him on her lap, and took care of him. —Ruth 4:16

Have you ever skinned your knee? Maybe you cried to Mom or another friendly person. You probably crawled up in her lap and let her comfort you. It didn't really fix anything, but you felt better. It's nice to be cared for. God's lap is available for you, and He does fix things.

WINNING BY LOSING

If anyone wants to be first, he must be last of all and servant of all. —Mark 9:35

"Second place is the first loser." Have you ever seen that T-shirt? One baseball manager used to say, "Nice guys finish last." We hear such talk around sports, but is it true? Jesus said that you don't win by being the top dog. You win by serving everybody else. That's a difficult idea to accept in this world, but it's God's way.

MAY 9

DISCIPLINE TIME

The one who will not use the rod hates his son, but the one who loves him disciplines him diligently.
—Proverbs 13:24

Confession time: I once put my daughter in a headlock and dragged her off a school bus kicking and screaming. Not exactly, but I thought I'd have to do that! She was being punished and I, mean old Dad, had to confront her defiance. It was difficult, but I knew I had to do it. God doesn't like to punish, but He does so out of love.

DO AS THEY SAY

children, obey your parents in the Lord,
because this is right. —Ephesians 6:1

"Why do I have to go to Sunday school? Dad doesn't go!" I argued. My mother stared at me.

"He's right," my father answered. "It's not fair. I'll go too."

Even if Dad hadn't been so brilliant that morning, I needed to obey Mom. Even when you think your parents are wrong, God wants you to honor and obey them.

DRIVING IN RUTS

Teach a youth about the way he should go; even when he is old he will not depart from it. —Proverbs 22:6

I drive my tractor along wooded trails. Years of travel have worn ruts in the ground. When I get into a rut, it's often tough to get out again. That's how life is. When you learn good habits, they're easy to keep. Bad habits are tough to break. Thank God and your family for all the good ruts they've gotten you into.

TRADITIONS: OLD OR NEW

Tell your children about it, and let your children tell their children, and their children the next generation. —Joel 1:3

Is it a tradition in your home to talk about how great God is? Do you read the Bible together? Do you pray? If so, that's wonderful. Somebody must have read today's verse. If you don't, why not start the tradition? Don't wait until you have kids of your own. Help your family start a tradition of worship today.

FEEL THE BURN!

No discipline seems enjoyable at the time, but painful. Later on, however, it yields the fruit of peace and righteousness to those who have been trained by it. —Hebrews 12:11

I'll admit it: I'm out of shape. When I do exercise, it's really going to hurt. I'll feel my chest burn. My legs will tremble and sweat will flow. Why would anybody put himself through that?

I know in the long run, exercise is good for me. I'll be strong and healthy. I'll learn to enjoy the burn. That's how it is with reading the Bible and prayer. Even if you don't feel like spending time with God, the more you do, the more you'll want to!

FAMILY RICHES

Teach them to your children and your
grandchildren. —Deuteronomy 4:9

My great grandfather served in the cavalry in the Civil War. He could ride a horse, but he couldn't read. He made sure my grandfather went to school. My grandfather made sure my father went to college. My father passed that treasure of education to me. If education is a treasure, how much more should you value the godly traditions of your family?

THE SOURCE OF WISDOM

For the LORD gives wisdom; from His
mouth come knowledge and understanding.
—Proverbs 2:6

I've been rearranging books for days. I'm a book lover
with hundreds of books at work and at home. I've learned a
great deal from my books, but the best thing I've learned is
that real wisdom, real knowledge, and real brilliance comes
from God—not from my books. When you read the Bible,
pray and ask God to give you wisdom and understanding.

DO YOU DO?

For I was hungry and you gave Me
something to eat; I was thirsty and
you gave Me something to drink;
I was a stranger and you took Me in.
—Matthew 25:35

You've probably heard someone say, "Do as I say, not as I do." What that person means is that he's not doing what he knows he should do.

Jesus doesn't want you to live like that. If you're a Christian, then you'll want to do good things for others. Don't just talk about it, do it!

HELP!

Each one of us must please his neighbor
for his good, in order to build him up.
—Romans 15:2

Have you ever had a friend who wore a cast because of a broken bone? You probably tried to help him by doing things like carrying his books, taking notes for him, or helping him walk up the stairs at school.

Jesus wants you to do things like that all the time. Pay attention to who needs help and give it to them.

TRUST AND OBEY

Seek first the kingdom of God and His righteousness, and all these things will be provided for you. —Matthew 6:33

Whenever a bird is hungry, it finds a worm in the dirt or a bug on a tree. It doesn't worry about whether or not the food will be there. It always is.

Just as God provides food for birds, He will also take care of you. Instead of worrying about your needs, trust God and focus your mind on doing what He wants you to do.

FIXING THE FAMILY

When Mary came to where Jesus was and
saw Him, she fell at His feet and
told Him, "Lord, if you had been here,
my brother would not have died!"
—John 11:32

Do your parents argue? Are your parents divorced? Does your family have money problems? Do you feel like life is out of control?

You can't fix all of your problems, but Jesus can do anything. Call on Him for help.

HELP AT HOME

He said to the disciple, "Here is your mother." And from that hour the disciple took her into his home. —John 19:27

The Bible tells you to honor your parents. This means that you respect them and try to help them in any way you can. Help your mom do the dishes without being asked. Take the trash out for your dad, or help him with a special project. By serving your parents, you are serving God.

YOUR SUBSTITUTE

While we were still helpless,
at the appointed moment, Christ died
for the ungodly. —Romans 5:6

Can you jump like Michael Jordan? Probably not. Can you skate like Tony Hawk? Not a chance!

Jesus did something that no human could ever do. He obeyed God perfectly, without ever sinning. That's why He's the only Son who deserves to be in God's family. Fortunately, though, you can be in God's family by trusting that Jesus did what you couldn't do.

HANG ON!

Trust in Him at all times, you people;
pour out your hearts before Him.
God is our refuge. —Psalm 62:8

Picture a movie scene in which a boy has fallen off the edge of a cliff, and the only thing saving him is the tree root he's hanging on to. Pretty scary situation, isn't it?

Sometimes you may feel like things can't get any worse, and there's no one who can help. Even when life seems hopeless, you can trust Jesus to save you.

ALL YOU NEED

My God will supply all your needs
according to His riches in glory in Christ
Jesus. —Philippians 4:19

When you go camping you only pack what is necessary.
You don't need to take your recliner or DVD player into the
woods. When you really think about it, there are a lot of
things in life that you could do without.

Knowing Jesus is something that you need more than
anything else. God will provide what you really need, and
the best thing He has provided is a Savior.

MIND YOUR BUSINESS

If anyone does not provide for his
own relatives, and especially for
his household, he has denied the faith
and is worse than an unbeliever.
—1 Timothy 5:8

As you grow up, remember that God has given you the job of taking care of your family. If you get married and have children, it will be your job to take care of them for the rest of your life. Even your parents may need help when they are older.

Begin thinking now about how you will obey God by providing for your family.

GOOD BOY

Share with the saints in their needs; pursue hospitality. —Romans 12:13

Has anyone ever done something nice for you for no apparent reason? Maybe he just suddenly surprised you with a friendly word or a kind action. Didn't that make you feel loved?

God wants you to help other Christians. You can show God's love by being nice, sharing, welcoming someone new, or by simply being generous.

CHOOSE JOY

Let your father and mother have joy, and let her who gave birth to you rejoice.
—Proverbs 23:25

When you make bad choices, your parents probably feel like they should have taught you better. But when you make good choices, they are glad that they helped you know right from wrong.

Whenever you have trouble deciding what to do, just ask yourself how Jesus would handle the situation. Usually, whatever choice pleases God will please your parents. And that's the right choice to make.

YES, MA'AM!

Honor your father and your mother so that you may have a long life in the land that the LORD your God is giving you.
—Exodus 20:12

Do you respect your parents by the way you talk to them and by promptly obeying them?

If not, remember that God commands you to respect them. He doesn't just suggest that you obey and respect. He actually demands it. Respecting and obeying your parents is one of the most important things you can do to honor God.

LISTEN LIKE JESUS

He went down with them and came to Nazareth and was obedient to them. His mother kept all these things in her heart.
—Luke 2:51

People at church talk a lot about Jesus being powerful and how He saves people from sin. But have you ever thought about Jesus being a child your age? That's right; at one time Jesus was a preteen!

Jesus faced tough problems, just like you do. But He always obeyed His parents, and you should too.

MAY 29

OBEY ALL THE WAY

children, obey your parents in everything,
for this is pleasing in the Lord.
—Colossians 3:20

Did you know that when you obey your parents you are also obeying God? God guides your parents, and then they guide you. That's how God helps you become the son that He wants you to be. So, the next time your parents give you a list of chores, remember that you are also doing those chores for God.

DO WHAT GOD SAYS

I was very glad to find some of your
children walking in truth, in keeping
with a command we have received
from the Father. —2 John 4

Did you know that sometimes newspapers print mistakes? When this happens, they have to print a correction so that the readers know the truth.

The Bible is the only book that doesn't have any mistakes. When it was first written, God made sure that the Bible said exactly what He wanted to say. Obey the Bible—it's 100 percent truth!

MAY 31

WHO'S THE BOSS?

If you love Me, you will keep
My commandments. —John 14:15

To be a Christian means that Jesus is Lord of your life.
Just like a servant wants to please his master, Christians
want to do what Jesus tells them to do in the Bible. He's
your Master.

Sometimes obeying Jesus is hard, but if you really love
Him you will still choose to obey Him.

THE REAL THING

The Son is the radiance of God's glory and the exact expression of His nature, sustaining all things by His powerful word. —Hebrews 1:3

Can you tell the difference between a real $1 bill and a counterfeit? As long as there has been money, people have been trying to make counterfeits that look like the real thing.

Jesus Christ came to the earth to show you God's love. Knowing Jesus is equal to knowing God. He is not just like God, He is God. He is the real thing!

PERFECT SACRIFICE

We do see Jesus . . . crowned with glory and honor because of His suffering in death. —Hebrews 2:9

Jesus Christ endured great pain at His death. He was beaten and mocked, and then He died a humiliating death on the cross. But His death wasn't the end. God proved He was satisfied with Jesus' sacrifice by raising Him from the dead and giving Him glory and honor. Jesus is alive today. His death provides forgiveness for you if you will admit, believe, and confess.

IT'S ALL ABOUT HIM!

All things exist for Him and through Him.
—Hebrews 2:10

Have your parents ever told you, "The world doesn't revolve around you"? They're right—it revolves around Jesus!

God created all things, and He alone gives life to creation. He did all of this to bring glory and honor to Himself. Everything that He created exists to show you His greatness. Take a look around and thank Him for being an awesome God!

THE FAMILY OF GOD

The One who sanctifies and those who
are sanctified all have one Father.
That is why Jesus is not ashamed
to call them brothers. —Hebrews 2:11

How do you feel when you hear that the Savior of the world has called you "brother"? Becoming a Christian means that you admit your sin, believe in Jesus' death and resurrection, and confess your faith in Jesus. You make Him your Lord and Savior. When you accept Him as Savior, He accepts you into His family.

BLESSED ASSURANCE

Since He Himself was tested and has suffered, He is able to help those who are tested. —Hebrews 2:18

Andrew was going through a tough time. His parents had just divorced, and he was moving to a new city. He felt like no one understood what he was going through.

This verse assures you that Jesus was tempted in the same way that you are tempted. Jesus understands exactly what you're going through and He wants to help you in your time of need.

MASTER PLAN

Now every house is built by someone,
but the One who built everything is God.
—Hebrews 3:4

A house cannot be built without an architect. The architect plans, designs, and oversees the construction of the house. Without proper plans, the house will never stand the test of time.

God is the architect of all creation. Everything is created by Him and according to His plans. His plans are perfect because He is perfect. God's plans never fail!

MIRROR, MIRROR

The word of God is living and effective and sharper than any double-edged sword.
—Hebrews 4:12

If you have spinach in your teeth or a hair that is standing up, a mirror helps you see what needs to be changed about your appearance.

God's Word is like a mirror. The Bible reveals God's truth for how you should live. It shows that everyone falls short of God's glory. It also teaches that everyone can be forgiven through the blood of Jesus.

FORGIVEN AND FORGOTTEN

Let us approach the throne of grace
with boldness, so that we may receive
mercy and find grace to help us at
the proper time. —Hebrews 4:16

When you are guilty of breaking the rules, do you go to your parents with boldness? Probably not! You're fearful because you're guilty and you know that there will be consequences.

If you are a Christian, Jesus has taken the punishment for your sin. Therefore, you can go to God without fear or shame because your sin is forgiven and forgotten!

LOVE HIM, LOVE OTHERS

God is not unjust; He will not forget
your work and the love you showed
for His Name. —Hebrews 6:10

Jesus taught that the greatest commandment is to love God with all your heart, soul, and mind. The second greatest commandment is to love your neighbor as yourself.

You are called to love and serve others. By serving, you show them that Jesus loves them and offers them eternal life. God sees your actions and will be faithful to reward your service.

DON'T HAVE TO SEE TO BELIEVE

Faith is the reality of what is hoped for,
the proof of what is not seen.
—Hebrews 11:1

Everyone places faith in something. When you sit in a chair, you have faith that the chair was properly constructed and will hold your weight.

God promises a heavenly reward to those who are committed to living for Him. Even though you cannot see the reward, faith helps you to live according to God's Word and to wait for His reward.

DADDY'S DISCIPLINE

Endure suffering as discipline: God is
dealing with you as sons. For what son is
there that a father does not discipline?
—Hebrews 12:7

The rule was "Don't play with Dad's tools." One day as
I played with his power drill, it fell to the ground and broke
into pieces. My father's discipline taught me a very valuable
lesson about obedience.

Sometimes life gives you lemons, but this verse reminds
you to trust that God loves you. He will use your struggle to
teach you a valuable lesson.

PURSUE PEACE

Pursue peace with everyone, and
holiness—without it no one will see
the Lord. —Hebrews 12:14

The world is watching to see if those who call themselves Christians act any different than those of the world.
It is important that you avoid fights and arguments so that
others can see the peace of God in you. You are called to
share Jesus with others through your words and actions.
Do others see Jesus in you?

UNCHANGING FRIEND

Jesus Christ is the same yesterday, today, and forever. —Hebrews 13:8

Life is full of changes. Some changes are good, but unfortunately some are bad. It is comforting to know that Jesus Christ never changes. He is perfect. He always has been, and He always will be. When everything around you is changing, Jesus Christ will always be the same amazing friend. Take some time to worship Jesus Christ for His unchanging love.

JUNE 14

SLOW TO SPEAK

My dearly loved brothers, understand this:
Everyone must be quick to hear, slow to
speak, and slow to anger, for man's anger
does not accomplish God's righteousness.
—James 1:19-20

Have you ever heard the phrase "put your foot in your mouth"? This means that you have said something without thinking about what you're really saying. It's easy to get angry and lose your cool. When this happens, nobody wins. Take the advice from this verse: listen carefully, pray before you speak, and keep your cool. When you do, others will see God through you!

DO YOU BELIEVE?

You believe that God is one;
you do well. The demons also
believe—and they shudder. —James 2:19

For several years, I thought that it was enough for me to just believe in God. But I was confused about what it meant to believe. I just believed that He existed, but I was not committed to following Him. Even the demons believe, but they are fearful because they are not obedient to Him.

Being a Christian means more than just believing in God; it means having faith in Jesus Christ as your Lord and Savior.

PRAYER BUDDY

Confess your sins to one another and pray for one another, so that you may be healed. —James 5:16

My baseball coach used to always tell me, "Practice makes perfect." During practice, he would point out the things that I needed to work on so that I could get better.

God has called His followers to hold one another accountable. Other believers can help you to grow in your faith, and you can do the same for them. Find a friend and pray for each other.

DO OVER

According to His great mercy, He has
given us a new birth into a living hope
through the resurrection of Jesus Christ
from the dead. —1 Peter 1:3

Have you ever messed up and wished you could just
have a "do over"? Jesus offers new life—eternal life—for
everyone who confesses Him as Savior and Lord. This new
life is like a "do over." Being born again means that your
sins are forgiven and you can live with the help of Jesus
Christ as your guide!

FAIR OR UNFAIR

You were called to this, because Christ also suffered for you, leaving you an example, so that you should follow in His steps. —1 Peter 2:21

"It's just not fair! The teacher is always picking on me." I was having a rough year with a teacher who just wasn't treating me fairly. I was very angry and having trouble dealing with the whole situation.

Jesus endured some pretty unfair treatment, yet He was always without sin. When you face unfair situations, remember to follow Jesus' example.

PASS THE PUNISHMENT

He Himself bore our sins in His body on the tree, so that, having died to sins, we might live for righteousness; you have been healed by His wounds.
—1 Peter 2:24

I had broken the living room lamp! When my parents got home, my older brother explained that he deserved to be punished since he was in charge while my parents were gone. My brother took the punishment that really should've been mine! Jesus Christ loves you so much that He died on the cross to take the punishment for your sin.

ARE YOU WASHED?

Christ also suffered for sins once for all, the righteous for the unrighteous, that He might bring you to God. —1 Peter 3:18

After mopping the kitchen floor, my mom tells me, "Don't walk across the floor!" She doesn't want dirty feet to get anywhere near her clean floor.

God is perfect, holy, and clean. Sin makes you imperfect, unholy, and dirty. You can't be near God unless you are made clean. The blood of Jesus has the power to wash away your sin! Are you washed?

GO AND TELL

The Lord does not delay His promise, as some understand delay, but is patient with you, not wanting any to perish but all to come to repentance. —2 Peter 3:9

Jesus promised that He would one day return to the earth. No one knows the time or the place, but He will keep His promise. In the meantime, He wants everyone to hear about Him and accept Him as Lord and Savior. Jesus wants you to tell others about Him so they can receive His grace and forgiveness. Whom will you tell?

DEEP ROOTS

Grow in the grace and knowledge of our Lord and Savior Jesus Christ.
—2 Peter 3:18

Last summer, a large tree fell in our yard. It only took a slight breeze to blow the tree down because the tree had very shallow roots. It had grown bigger and bigger, but its roots never got deeper than the surface. Studying God's Word will help you grow deeper in your understanding of the Savior so that you can withstand the devil's temptations.

STOP FOOLING YOURSELF

If we say, "We have no sin,"
we are deceiving ourselves,
and the truth is not in us.
—1 John 1:8

It's hard to admit when you're wrong. That's probably because no one likes to feel the shame that comes with being wrong. When it comes to sin, you can't say that you do not sin. God's Word is clear that everyone falls short of His glory. Instead of denying that you're wrong, try confessing to God and seeking His forgiveness.

CONFESS AND CHANGE

If we confess our sins, He is faithful and righteous to forgive us our sins and to cleanse us from all unrighteousness.
—1 John 1:9

One day, the teacher caught my friend cheating on his class work. He admitted that he had done so and told the teacher he was sorry. The next day, he was caught doing the exact same thing.

Confessing your sin means that you admit it to God and you change your ways to follow Him. When you do, He is faithful to forgive.

JUNE 25

ADOPTED BY A KING

Look at how great a love the Father has given us that we should be called God's children. And we are! —1 John 3:1

Have you ever imagined what it would be like to be part of a royal family? As the son of a king, you would have riches and treasures that all belong to you. Now imagine the treasures that come with being a child of God, the Most High King. Thank Him for adopting you into His royal family.

OVERFLOW OF LOVE

We love because He first loved us.
—1 John 4:19

When I pour soda into a glass, I have a tendency to pour too much, and then it bubbles over onto the counter. This is called an overflow. When you think about all the love that God has shown you, can you contain it all? God's love should make you so full that you overflow with love for others.

HE HEARS YOU

This is the confidence we have before Him: Whenever we ask anything according to His will, He hears us. —1 John 5:14

Will God give you anything you ask Him for? This verse does not say that God will give you everything you ask, but it does show something about how God answers prayer. God promises that His plan will be done. So when you ask for things that are part of God's plan, you can be sure that He hears and answers those prayers.

SOUVENIR FROM HEAVEN

The Son of God has come and has given us understanding so that we may know the true One. —1 John 5:20

When my parents go on vacation, they always bring back a souvenir for me. It's a great way for me to learn about the places they visited. Jesus Christ came to the earth to show you more about who God is and how much He loves you. Jesus is God's gift to help know Him.

THAT BELONGS TO GOD

Little children, guard yourselves
from idols. —1 John 5:21

An idol isn't just a golden statue of a cow; an idol is anything that you love more than God. It can be money, appearances, friends—or a million other things. These are not all bad things, but be careful that they don't become more important than God. Your heart belongs to God; don't give it away to anything else.

HAVE MERCY

Have mercy on those who doubt.
—Jude 22

Does every one of your friends believe in God? If not, how do you treat those who doubt Him?

This verse is a reminder of how you are to treat those who struggle to believe in God. God wants you to show them mercy and understanding. In doing so, you can open the door to share the gospel with them and with others.

WHY SUNDAY?

I was in the Spirit on the Lord's day,
and I heard a loud voice behind me
like a trumpet. —Revelation 1:10

Have you ever wondered why Christians gather on Sunday? It's because Jesus was raised from the dead on a Sunday! Jesus' followers have always come together for worship on this day to celebrate His resurrection. The book of Revelation opens with the apostle John having a vision on a Sunday—the Lord's Day. Do you prioritize the Lord's Day in your heart? Are you ready to gather and worship with God's people this Sunday?

JULY 2

LONG LOST LOVE

But I have this against you: you have
abandoned the love you had at first.
—Revelation 2:4

Ever outgrown something or thought, I'm no longer interested in or excited about this? Well, Jesus once told a group of believers something that should send chills up any Christian's spine: "You've outgrown Me." You see, it's so easy to start off strong in your walk with Jesus, only to fizzle out over time. Have you fizzled? Has your heart grown cold to His love? Friend, don't abandon Jesus—the treasure of the believer's heart.

GOSPEL MATH

I know your affliction and poverty,
yet you are rich. I know the slander
of those who say they are Jews and
are not, but are a synagogue of Satan.
—Revelation 2:9

Is Jesus confused here? First He tells these believers that they're persecuted and poor, then that they're rich! So, which is it? Amazingly, it's both.

Here's some simple math for you to consider today: Jesus + nothing = everything. If you have a personal relationship with Jesus, then you have everything you need. You are truly rich.

Remember: Jesus + nothing = everything.

KNOCK, KNOCK

Listen! I stand at the door and knock. If anyone hears My voice and opens the door, I will come in to him and have dinner with him, and he with Me.
—Revelation 3:20

Jesus spoke these words to a group of believers who didn't seem to have room for Him. Sounds strange, right? But you know, we can be the same way. We can clutter our lives with so many things—even good things—that we forget about the best thing. We can forget about Him. Is Jesus living in your heart, or have you shut Him out of your life? He's pursuing a relationship with you today. He's knocking. Will you let Him in?

NOT LIKE YOU

Each of the four living creatures had six wings; they were covered with eyes around and inside. Day and night they never stop, saying: Holy, holy, holy, Lord God, the Almighty, who was, who is, and who is coming. —Revelation 4:8

God isn't like you. That may sound like a bad thing, but it's actually great news. You see, humans are unholy, sinful, and rebellious. But God isn't. He's perfect. He's in a league of His own. It's precisely because He's so different, so unique—so holy—that He could become the solution to the problem we created. The good news is that the holy One made a way through His Son for unholy ones (you and me!) to be forgiven and accepted by Him forever.

WORTH-SHIP

Our Lord and God, You are worthy to receive glory and honor and power, because You have created all things, and because of Your will they exist and were created. —Revelation 4:11

What's the most valuable thing you have? What in your life is most precious to you? In this verse we catch a glimpse of eternity, when those in heaven will celebrate the most valuable being—God. His worth will be displayed, and your soul—if you're His child through faith in Jesus—will be satisfied. If you were to list what your heart cherishes most, would God make the cut? Do you live like He is worth your worship, your life?

LIFTIN' UP THE LAMB

I heard every creature in heaven, on earth, under the earth, on the sea, and everything in them say: Blessing and honor and glory and dominion to the One seated on the throne, and to the Lamb, forever and ever! —Revelation 5:13

Does it sound a bit weird to you that believers will be forever worshiping a lamb? In the Old Testament, God's people sacrificed lambs to pay for their sin. In the New Testament, however, Jesus is the final sacrifice, the final offering—the promised "Lamb of God" who takes away sin once and for all. Is your guilt covered by faith in Jesus' blood? Will you be counted among God's people when they gather in heaven to celebrate the Lamb?

WORSHIP: ANYTIME, ANYWHERE

The four living creatures said, "Amen,"
and the elders fell down and worshiped.
—Revelation 5:14

What is worship? Just a Sunday thing? Did you know that, according to the Bible, worship isn't primarily an event? It's a lifestyle. It's meant to shape everything you do as a follower of Jesus.

What this means is that you can worship Jesus literally anywhere. So whatever you're doing today, ask God to help you treasure Him above all else. Friend, you can't love anything rightly until you love Jesus more.

JULY 9

HUH?

Then I saw the Lamb open one of the seven seals, and I heard one of the four living creatures say with a voice like thunder, "Come!" I looked, and there was a white horse. The horseman on it had a bow; a crown was given to him, and he went out as a victor to conquer.
—Revelation 6:1–2

Some passages in Scripture are hard to understand, aren't they? This is probably one of them. Why did God put difficult texts in His Word? One reason was to humble us. Verses like these are good reminders that we don't know everything; only God does. Also, they lead us to study, pray, and depend on the Holy Spirit to help us grasp what we can't figure out on our own. That's always a good thing.

JULY 10

EVERY TRIBE AND NATION

*After this I looked, and there was a
vast multitude from every nation, tribe,
people, and language, which no one could
number, standing before the throne and
before the Lamb. They were robed in
white with palm branches in their hands.
—Revelation 7:9*

What's the language of heaven? English? Spanish?
Chinese? German? Believe it or not, the Bible says that
God will be celebrated in every human language. Heaven's
population will be magnificently diverse. Jesus' followers
from every culture, skin color, background, and nation will
gather together by grace.

We're not going to all look or sound the same! God's
glory will be reflected by our beautiful differences. Aren't
you excited?

SING TO THE KING

All the angels stood around the throne, the elders, and the four living creatures, and they fell facedown before the throne and worshiped God. —Revelation 7:11

Have you ever reflected on what it means that God is King? He's the King of the universe; is He also your King? Have you bowed your knee to Him, pledging allegiance to His loving rule over your life?

Sin is making yourself king. Conversion to Christ, however, involves a kingdom transfer—getting moved by grace from the realm of self-rule to the realm of Christ-rule. Have you embraced Jesus as King?

JULY 12

GOT ACCESS?

For this reason they are before the throne of God, and they serve Him day and night in His sanctuary. The One seated on the throne will shelter them. —Revelation 7:15

"For this reason." What reason? Well, in the previous verse we read that these believers' robes were washed and whitened by "the blood of the Lamb." So it's for that reason—because their moral filth has been cleansed through Jesus' death in their place—that they can boldly approach God's heavenly throne.

Has your Maker given you access to His throne? If you're relying on Jesus alone, then He has. The only question is, are you?

CRY NO MORE

They will no longer hunger; they will no longer thirst; the sun will no longer strike them, nor will any heat. For the Lamb who is at the center of the throne will shepherd them; He will guide them to springs of living waters, and God will wipe away every tear from their eyes.
—Revelation 7:16–17

What would it be like to never again experience hunger, thirst, pain, or sadness?

What we have here is a precious promise for every believer who suffers, every Christ follower who despairs, every child of God whose life is filled with pain. How amazing to think that God Himself will personally wipe away the tears—fully and finally—from all who have embraced His Son! Have you?

THAT SMELLS GOOD

The smoke of the incense, with the
prayers of the saints, went up in the
presence of God from the angel's hand.
—Revelation 8:4

The Bible describes your prayers as pleasing incense rising to God's throne. Think about that. Whenever you approach God through Jesus in prayer, a fragrant aroma ascends to Him.

No humble request of yours, then, is ever wasted or lost. Ever. God loves listening to you. Have you spoken with Him lately?

HEAD COUNT

Then I was given a measuring reed like a rod, with these words: "Go and measure God's sanctuary and the altar, and count those who worship there."
—Revelation 11:1

The apostle John just received orders to take a "head count" of everyone who loves and praises Jesus. Does that include you? Have you turned away from worshipping other things—God-substitutes—and started worshipping Jesus instead? If you have, then does your life reflect this radical shift? Do you spend your time treasuring God, or do you waste it idolizing lesser things? Will you be counted among God's worshippers?

PICK A TEAM

The seventh angel blew his trumpet, and
there were loud voices in heaven saying:
The kingdom of the world has become the
kingdom of our Lord and of His Messiah,
and He will reign forever and ever!
—Revelation 11:15

What's the best movie ending you've ever seen? It probably had something to do with good guys winning and bad guys losing. The Bible ends with a preview of how the world ends. God's unrepentant enemies are conquered, and God's uncontested rule becomes reality at last. Are you on the winning team? If you're relying simply on what Jesus has done for you, then you'll share in His victory by His grace.

KINGLY KINDNESS

The 24 elders, who were seated before God on their thrones, fell facedown and worshiped God, saying: We thank You, Lord God, the Almighty, who is and who was, because You have taken Your great power and have begun to reign.
—Revelation 11:16–17

So many people in this world use their power in harmful, even cruel, ways. But unlike anyone else, God alone mingles perfect power with perfect goodness. His power doesn't trump His goodness, and His goodness doesn't trump His power. That's why the believers in this verse thank God for His powerful kingship. When the perfectly loving King is on the throne, it's good news for humble sinners!

DECISION TIME

The nations were angry, but Your wrath has come. The time has come for the dead to be judged and to give the reward to Your servants the prophets, to the saints, and to those who fear Your name, both small and great, and the time has come to destroy those who destroy the earth.
—Revelation 11:18

This is a shocking verse. God will do one of two things to every human: deliver or destroy. If you've received Jesus, trusting Him alone to rescue you from God's judgment, then you'll forever enjoy His grace. If you reject Him, choosing to live for yourself instead, then you'll forever experience His wrath. Who'll be the leader and treasure of your life?

VICTORY IS COMING SOON

Then war broke out in heaven: Michael
and his angels fought against the dragon.
The dragon and his angels also fought, but
he could not prevail, and there was no
place for them in heaven any longer.
—Revelation 12:7-8

At the end of history—at the end of time—there is going to be a great cosmic war. And you know what? We've already been told how it's going to turn out! We know the final score.

The devil and his demons will be decisively defeated, once and for all. God and His angels will stand victorious, along with all who are on His side by faith in His Son.

Will that include you?

WHERE'S YOUR JOY?

Therefore rejoice, you heavens, and you who dwell in them! —Revelation 12:12

Have you ever realized that God orders you to delight in Him? And it's not just some suggestion, either. It's a command—one having to do not with fleeting feelings of happiness, but with deep and lasting satisfaction in Jesus.

So rejoice, delight, and be glad in God! Enjoy your Savior. There's simply nothing on this earth more satisfying than Him.

REDEMPTION SONG

They sang a new song before the throne
and before the four living creatures
and the elders, but no one could learn
the song except the 144,000 who
had been redeemed from the earth.
—Revelation 14:3

If your dog bit you and ran away, would you pay to get him back from the animal shelter? That's a tough decision.

God made you and owns you. Because of your sin, however, He had to pay in order to get you back. And pay He did! On the cross, Jesus sacrificed His life to bring lost sinners like you back to God.

Have you been redeemed by faith in His blood?

THE DOORWAY

Then I heard a voice from heaven saying, "Write: The dead who die in the Lord from now on are blessed." "Yes," says the Spirit, "let them rest from their labors, for their works follow them!" —Revelation 14:13

For the believer in Jesus, death isn't a wall; it's a door. It marks the beginning—not the end—of life. You see, when a Christian dies, his soul goes to be with the Lord and he begins to experience everlasting enjoyment of the King.

This life is the closest an unbeliever will ever get to heaven. And this life is the closest a believer will ever get to hell. Think about that.

THE PLEASURE OF PRAISE

I also saw something like a sea of glass mixed with fire, and those who had won the victory over the beast, his image, and the number of his name, were standing on the sea of glass with harps from God. —Revelation 15:2

It's easy to assume pleasure and praise are totally different things, isn't it? But did you know that according to the Bible, pleasure and praise go together like milk and cookies? God built you—designed you—to find ultimate pleasure in knowing and loving Him. You see, the more you enjoy Jesus, the more you'll exalt Him. And the more you exalt Him, the more you'll enjoy Him. So praise Him for His glory, and praise Him for your good!

RIGHT IN HIS SIGHT?

Great and awe-inspiring are Your works,
Lord God, the Almighty; righteous and
true are Your ways, King of the Nations.
—Revelation 15:3

All of God's ways are righteous. But how can He remain righteous when He forgives the guilty? Think about it—if a human judge were to release a convicted criminal just because he "loved" him, what'd happen? That unjust judge would lose his job!

How can God forgive sin and still remain righteous? Answer: the cross. There, God's justice was satisfied because Jesus was punished for sin. His mercy is for you.

THE COMEBACK

"Look, I am coming like a thief. The one who is alert and remains clothed so that he may not go around naked and people see his shame is blessed."
—Revelation 16:15

Jesus came, and He's coming back. Are you ready for His return? Are you awake and alert? Are you excited to see Him?

If you haven't given your life to Jesus, the clock is ticking. You know you aren't guaranteed next year, next month, or even next week, right? Have you been reconnected to God? Have you embraced Jesus by faith—relying on Him alone to forgive your sin and make peace with your Maker?

WHERE'S YOUR NAME?

Those who live on the earth whose names have not been written in the book of life from the foundation of the world will be astonished when they see the beast that was, and is not, and will be present again. —Revelation 17:8

What's "the book of life"? It's a book that lists every human who will enjoy eternal life with God. It's a permanent record of all who repent from sin, rely on Jesus, and are redeemed by God. Is your name written in this book of life? If you trust in Jesus as Savior and follow Him as Lord, it is.

Is Jesus your Savior and Lord?

READY OR NOT, HERE HE COMES

The sound of harpists, musicians, flutists, and trumpeters will never be heard in you again; no craftsman of any trade will ever be found in you again; the sound of a mill will never be heard in you again.
—Revelation 18:22

Things that seem so permanent in this world won't last forever. For those who refuse to trust and follow Jesus, the sounds of everyday business and enjoyment of life in this world are passing away. For unbelievers, the sounds of laughter and happiness in this world will one day stop. Suddenly. When King Jesus returns, everyone who isn't connected to Him by faith will be justly punished. Forever. Are you ready for the return of the King?

LIFT THOSE EYES

Hallelujah! Salvation, glory, and power belong to our God. —Revelation 19:1

"Follow your heart!" "Believe in yourself!" "You can do anything!" Ever heard that? It's a very popular thing these days to look within yourself and be impressed. But Scripture says that true joy, freedom, and life is only found when you look away from yourself to God. Salvation is His, not yours. Glory is His, not yours. Power is His, not yours. So celebrate Him, not yourself! Shift your focus to Jesus—the only One worthy of it.

LIFT HIM UP!

Praise our God, all His slaves,
who fear Him, both small and great!
—Revelation 19:5

Got lots of friends? Does everybody seem to like you? Does everything seem to go your way? If so, you're commanded to do one thing: praise God! Do you struggle to make friends? Does everybody seem to ignore you? Does everything seem to go wrong? If so, you're commanded to do one thing: praise God! No matter how you feel, He is worth your worship. What matters isn't what others think of you; it's what you think of Him.

SAVE THE DATE

Let us be glad, rejoice, and give Him glory, because the marriage of the Lamb has come, and His wife has prepared herself. —Revelation 19:7

Ever watched a bride walk down the aisle to her groom? Every Christian wedding is a small picture of that ultimate marriage at the end of time when Jesus' purified people will be united to Him forever.

Right now, it's as if Christ and His church are engaged. The wedding is sure, but it hasn't happened yet. And if you've been purified through faith in Jesus, then you won't just be invited, it'll be your wedding day, too.

COMING SOON: NEWNESS

Then the One seated on the throne said, "Look! I am making everything new." He also said, "Write, because these words are faithful and true." And He said to me, "It is done! I am the Alpha and the Omega, the Beginning and the End. I will give water as a gift to the thirsty from the spring of life." —Revelation 21:5-6

Ever been extremely sad? Ever felt lonely? If not, you will. This fallen world is filled with disappointment, heartbreak, sadness, suffering, and death. But that's not the end of the story! There's a day coming when everything broken will be remade, everything wrong will be righted, and everything sad will become untrue. He'll make all things new.

FRIEND OF GOD

The LORD spoke with Moses face to face,
just as a man speaks with his friend.
—Exodus 33:11

Have you ever thought of God as your friend?

Moses got to experience a close friendship with God. His close relationship allowed him to hear from God and present his needs to Him. Through the blood of Jesus Christ, you too can have a friendship with the heavenly Father. The God of the universe wants to be your friend!

BROTHERLY LOVE

Jonathan committed himself to David, and loved him as much as he loved himself.
—1 Samuel 18:1

King Saul was jealous of David. His jealousy even made him attempt to kill David. Saul's son, Jonathan, was a friend of David. Jonathan protected David and loved him as if they were brothers.

True friendship means that you treat the other person with respect and love. That's brotherly love!

COMFORT & CARE

They met together to go and sympathize with him and comfort him. —Job 2:11

"Michael really needs you to be his friend right now. He has had a really rough week," my mom said to me after the funeral. My best friend had just lost his grandfather. He needed friends to pray for him and lift him up during this rough time.

When your friends go through hard times, look for ways to comfort them.

QUALITY VS. QUANTITY

A man with many friends may be harmed, but there is a friend who stays closer than a brother. —Proverbs 18:24

My baseball card collection has over 3,000 cards and is worth about $800. My friend Jeremy owns one baseball card, yet his collection is worth almost $3,000! His card is far more valuable than my entire collection!

A great friend is someone who encourages you to live for Jesus every day. Many friends are good, but one great friend is much better.

TELL THE WORLD!

You will be My witnesses in Jerusalem, in all Judea and Samaria, and to the ends of the earth. —Acts 1:8

As a Christian, you have been given the power and boldness to tell the story of Jesus! This Scripture speaks of four locations: city, state, country, and then the world. Your mission is to spread the good news to your neighborhood, your state, your country, and the rest of the world! It's a big job, but you can do it with God's help!

AUGUST 6

A FRIENDLY VISIT

A friend loves at all times, and
a brother is born for a difficult time.
—Proverbs 17:17

Have you ever heard of a guy named Onesiphorus? When the apostle Paul was imprisoned in Rome, he was desperate for a friend to visit him. Onesiphorus risked his own freedom and his own life to go and visit Paul. Paul had a friend when he most needed him.

Are you there for your friends in good times and bad times?

MAN'S BEST FRIEND

A despairing man should receive loyalty from his friends. —Job 6:14

When I caught the flu a few years ago, I literally couldn't get up off the couch. I was too sick to do anything. Through the entire illness, my dog stayed by my side and kept me company. It was as if she knew how badly I was feeling and wanted to make it better.

You can learn a lesson in loyalty from man's best friend!

AUGUST 8

ROTTEN APPLE

The one who walks with the wise will become wise, but a companion of fools will suffer harm. —Proverbs 13:20

Do you know what happens when you put a perfectly good apple next to a rotten apple? The rotten apple continues to wither and rot, and eventually it causes the good apple to also become rotten.

Just like the apples, choosing friends with bad character can ruin good character. Make sure you choose your friends wisely!

AUGUST 9

WALK UPRIGHT

Watch the blameless and observe
the upright, for the man of peace
will have a future. —Psalm 37:37

Chad was my best friend during middle school. He was a few years older than me, and he was a great role model. He loved God and faithfully lived for Him. As I grew older, I learned to love God and walk with Him because I watched the example Chad set for me. Find an upright friend to help you grow closer to God.

PRAY FOR A FRIEND

I vow that I will not sin against the LORD by ceasing to pray for you.
—1 Samuel 12:23

Do you pray for your friends? One of the greatest things that you can do for your friends is to pray for them daily. Your friends face struggles just like you, and the best way to be their friend is to ask God to help and comfort them. Your prayers can be a great encouragement to a friend.

KEEP IT UNDER CONTROL

Don't make friends with an angry man, and don't be a companion of a hot-tempered man. —Proverbs 22:24

Even though Anthony was always getting into trouble, Daniel thought it would be cool to be his friend. He thought that being friends with Anthony would bring instant popularity. Instead, Daniel found himself caught up in Anthony's schemes, fighting, and breaking rules.

Choose your friends carefully.

THE PERFECT AGE

Do not say, "I am only a youth, for you will go to everyone I send you to and speak whatever I tell you." —Jeremiah 1:7

Have you ever heard the saying "age is just a number"? This is definitely true when it comes to serving God.

It doesn't matter if you are young or old; God has given you all the necessary knowledge and power to serve Him. Even as a preteen, you can boldly tell others the story of Jesus Christ.

IT'S A TRAP!

My son, if sinners entice you,
don't be persuaded. —Proverbs 1:10

I love cookies. I love them so much that it's hard for me to eat just one. I have to work really hard to practice self-control and not eat the entire box of cookies!

We all face temptations. When you are tempted, stand your ground and practice self-control so that you do not fall into the trap of sin.

WATCH YOUR MOUTH

LORD, set up a guard for my mouth;
keep watch at the door of my lips.
—Psalm 141:3

As soon as the words left Jacob's mouth, he knew that he shouldn't have said such foul words. He knew better than to curse, but now he had to face the consequences for what he said.

The most powerful muscle in your body is your tongue. Your words can hurt others and yourself. You must learn to control the tongue!

AUGUST 15

STICKS AND STONES

A contrary man spreads conflict,
and a gossip separates close friends.
—Proverbs 16:28

Have you heard the saying, "Sticks and stones may break my bones, but words will never hurt me." This saying just isn't true because words can really hurt.

A friend is someone you can really trust, but gossip tears down trust. When you let gossip come from your mouth, it can hurt others and ruin friendships.

WALK AWAY

A fool's displeasure is known at once,
but whoever ignores an insult is sensible.
—Proverbs 12:16

Chloe looked at him and said, "Boys are stupid!" William was hurt by her words. He could've said mean things back to her, but he knew that would only make the situation worse. Instead, William decided to just walk away.

When others use their words to hurt you, the best thing to do is walk away.

KEEP THE PEACE

The peacemakers are blessed, for they will be called sons of God. —Matthew 5:9

I have a friend who is a farmer. He learned to be a farmer because his father, grandfather, and great-grandfather were also farmers. Each generation had passed on everything needed to be an excellent farmer.

God the Father is Peace. As a Christian, He has given you that peace. God has passed on to you everything needed to be a peacemaker.

PROMISES, PROMISES

Let your word "yes" be "yes," and your "no" be "no." —Matthew 5:37

Have you ever said, "I promise," while crossing your fingers? By crossing your fingers, it means that you don't plan to keep that promise! These words from Jesus urge you to keep your promises. If you say you will do something, then you should always follow through and actually do it. Are you keeping your word?

WONDERFUL WORKS

Sing to Him, sing praise to Him;
tell about all His wonderful works!
—Psalm 105:2

Did you know that many U.S. presidents have a presidential library? Millions of people visit these huge collections of pictures and documents that tell everything a president did while he was in office.

God has done so much more than any U.S. president! God's library is His creation. It's all His.

THE EXTRA MILE

If anyone forces you to go one mile,
go with him two. —Matthew 5:41

The Roman soldiers of Jesus' time would often force people to carry their heavy equipment for up to a mile. Many people hated the soldiers for this cruel practice. Jesus taught them to set an example by doing what the soldier required plus an extra mile!

When there is a need, set an example by doing even more than you have to do.

AUGUST 21

MIRROR, MIRROR

Why do you look at the speck in your brother's eye but don't notice the log in your own eye? —Matthew 7:3

Have you ever gone a day without looking at yourself in a mirror? It's normal to check your appearance before going out. Jesus reminds us that we also need to daily check out our hearts and our actions for sin. Instead of focusing on the faults of others, examine your own sins and ask God for help in those areas.

ON GOD'S TEAM

Walk worthy of the calling you have received, with all humility and gentleness, with patience, accepting one another in love. —Ephesians 4:1-2

"Stop running in the hall," said the 7th grade football coach. He knew it was me because I was wearing my football jersey! He told me that wearing that jersey meant I represented the whole team, so I'd better follow the rules.

As a Christian, you have been called to live in a way that represents God and His greatness!

LEND A HAND

Carry one another's burdens; in this way
you will fulfill the law of Christ.
—Galatians 6:2

Seth was having a hard time carrying his books and walking with crutches. Connor decided to serve Seth by carrying his books for the rest of the day. Seth was very grateful for the help!

Jesus has commanded you to love your neighbor the way you love yourself. See a friend in need? Lend a hand.

THE OVERFLOW

No foul language is to come from your mouth, but only what is good for building up someone in need. —Ephesians 4:29

If you pour muddy water into a cup, do you know what will overflow out of that same cup? Of course you would get muddy water!

If you allow foul language to go into your heart, then it will eventually overflow out of your mouth. Protect yourself by keeping away from conversations that don't encourage you to grow closer to God.

BEFORE THE SUN GOES DOWN

Be angry and do not sin. Don't let the sun go down on your anger. —Ephesians 4:26

Did you know that it's OK to get angry? It's not a sin to get angry, but it can be a sin based on how you react.

When you get angry, the proper response is gentleness. Go and talk calmly with the other person and resolve the conflict immediately. Ask God for help so that you can respond to anger without sinning.

ONE DAY

My mouth will tell about Your
righteousness and Your salvation
all day long. —Psalm 71:15

It's so hard for me to sleep on Christmas Eve. I stay up all night thinking about the presents, the food, and the fun. I just can't get the excitement out of my head!

It's even more exciting to think about being with God in heaven. God promises that all believers will one day join Him for all of eternity. That will be a really big celebration.

FOOLISH FIGHTS

Reject foolish and ignorant disputes,
knowing that they breed quarrels.
—2 Timothy 2:23

The feud between the Hatfields and McCoys is probably the most famous fight in history. These families fought with each other for more than 35 years! The feud started with two men arguing over who got to keep a pig!

Avoid foolish fights and arguments so that you don't get caught up in an even bigger feud!

SHOW THEM JESUS

Don't neglect to show hospitality.
—Hebrews 13:2

Hunter, a 5th grader, stands at the front doors every Sunday and welcomes each kid with a high-five. Kids love coming to church because they know Hunter will welcome them!

Hunter is showing others the love of Jesus through the gift of hospitality. Showing hospitality is a great way for you to tell others about Jesus Christ!

WHO IS #1?

Everyone should look out not only for his own interests, but also for the interests of others. —Philippians 2:4

Have you ever heard someone say, "I'm just looking out for #1"? What they mean is that they are only concerned about themselves and not with the feelings or needs of others. God calls you to live differently. He commands you to love others and to look out for their needs. Who will you look out for as #1—yourself or others?

AUGUST 30

PERFECT STRANGER

Dear friend, you are showing faithfulness
by whatever you do for the brothers,
especially when they are strangers.
—3 John 5

Zach's friends asked him, "Why would you go feed a meal to a bunch of strangers?" "We feed them so that we can serve Jesus and tell them His story," Zach responded.

You serve Jesus Christ by serving others. Even when you do something for a stranger, you can be confident that you are really doing it for Jesus Christ.

BROTHERS AND SISTERS

Dear friend, I pray that you may prosper in every way and be in good health physically just as you are spiritually.
—3 John 2

Even if they weren't getting along, Ben prayed that God would keep his brother healthy and safe every night. Ben prayed for his brother because they are family.

All believers are a part of the family of God. You should pray that God would be with your brothers and sisters in Christ and keep them safe because you are all in God's family.

SEPTEMBER 1

LIVE WITH PURPOSE

God created man in His own image;
He created him in the image of God;
He created them male and female.
—Genesis 1:27

Notice the word *created* in this passage. Why is it repeated three times?

This word emphasizes God's power. It also shows how important humans are—you were intentionally created in the image of God with a unique purpose. Today, focus on living for Him and His purpose for you.

THE LOVE OF GOD

The LORD God made clothing out of
skins for Adam and his wife,
and He clothed them. —Genesis 3:21

Adam and Eve were caught red-handed in their sin. Despite their disobedience, God still provided for them.

God loves you and He will always provide for you. He even provided a way to be with Him for eternity: through a personal relationship with Jesus Christ.

MISSION: NOT IMPOSSIBLE

Then the LORD said to Noah, "Enter the ark, you and all your household, for I have seen that you alone are righteous before Me in this generation." —Genesis 7:1

God told Noah to bring two of every animal on the ark with him. Sounds impossible, right?

Sometimes walking with God and doing the right thing is hard, but take encouragement from the story of Noah. God will always be with you in every moment, even if it seems impossible.

MAKE THE SACRIFICE

The LORD said to Abram: "Go out from your land, your relatives, and your father's house to the land that I will show you." —Genesis 12:1

Abram made a sacrifice: He followed God's command to leave almost everything he knew, and he didn't know if God would keep His promise.

If you live for God, you will have to make tough choices. But remember that God loves you and always has a perfect plan for you.

TOUGH CHOICES

Abram believed the LORD, and He credited it to him as righteousness. —Genesis 15:6

Abram was old and childless, but God said that he would have as many children as the stars. Although it seemed unbelievable, Abram chose to have faith in God.

Your faith and walk with God is also a choice. Today, choose to glorify God in everything you do.

PEACEFUL CONFRONTATION

He said, "Don't do this evil, my brothers."
—Genesis 19:7

In this passage, Lot put himself in serious danger and peacefully stood up against an evil mob to save three visitors.

Sometimes you may have to stand up to other people (like bullies) to help someone else. Remember to confront others peacefully and act out of love.

GOD'S GUIDANCE

"LORD, God of my master Abraham," he prayed, "give me success today, and show kindness to my master Abraham."
—Genesis 24:12

Abraham's servant was in the right place at the right time. He did everything he could to find a wife for Isaac, but he knew that he still needed God's help.

No matter what happens today, remember to always ask for God's guidance and always thank Him.

NEVER GIVE UP

Jacob worked seven years for Rachel, and they seemed like only a few days to him because of his love for her.
—Genesis 29:20

Jacob worked seven years of physical labor in order to marry Rachel, but when it was finished he was tricked into working seven more!

Have you ever wanted to give up on something? If so, reflect on your attitude in that situation and take encouragement from the story of Jacob.

FAMILY REUNION

> Esau ran to meet him, hugged him, threw his arms around him, and kissed him. Then they wept. —Genesis 33:4

Jacob and Esau were once adversaries, even to the point of death. But when they came together in this passage, they were able to peacefully reunite.

Are you currently angry at any friends or family members? Today, meditate on this passage and pray for God's help to forgive and forget.

HUMILITY

Then Joseph had a dream. When he told it to his brothers, they hated him even more. —Genesis 37:5

Joseph had two dreams that showed him ruling over his family. When he explained the dreams, he told the truth, but he did it out of pride.

If you excel at anything, remember to be humble and thank God for His blessings. Today, remember where all your blessings come from.

253

GOD'S PURPOSE

The LORD was with Joseph and
extended kindness to him. He granted him
favor in the eyes of the prison warden.
—Genesis 39:21

Up to this point in Genesis, Joseph had experienced multiple hardships, including betrayal by his own brothers. But God was still in control and everything happened for a reason.

Today, give God control. No matter what happens (good and bad), He loves you and has a purpose for your life.

GOD'S PERFECT TIMING

Two years later Pharaoh had a dream: He was standing beside the Nile.
—GENESIS 41:1

Joseph was in jail for two years before God gave Pharaoh a dream. Despite his circumstances, Joseph never turned his back on God.

What would you do if you were Joseph? Would you give up hope? Today, remember that God's timing is perfect and that He is always in control.

REMEMBER GOD'S BLESSINGS

And the second son he named Ephraim, meaning, "God has made me fruitful in the land of my affliction." —Genesis 41:52

In 13 years, Joseph went from a foreign slave to the world's second most powerful man. No matter what happened, He always remembered God's blessings.

Today, take notice of how God has blessed you. You can't always control what happens in your life, but you can control how you react to it.

FORGIVE AND FORGET

Joseph kissed each of his brothers
as he wept, and afterward his brothers
talked with him. —Genesis 45:15

Joseph showed true forgiveness in this scene. Not only did he forgive his brothers (who once plotted to kill him), but he provided them with food and a new place to live.

How can you show forgiveness in your life? Today, ask God for the strength to forgive and forget.

KEEP HOPE ALIVE

Israel said to Joseph, "I never expected
to see your face again, but now God has
even let me see your offspring."
—Genesis 48:11

It seems that Jacob (Israel) gave up hope of ever seeing
Joseph again. But God surprised and blessed him in more
ways than one.

God is the creator of all things, there's nothing that He
can't do. Trust Him today—you may be surprised at what
He does in your life.

GET FOCUSED

John himself had a camel-hair garment with a leather belt around his waist, and his food was locusts and wild honey.
—Matthew 3:4

John the Baptist was a prophet who told others about Jesus. He wasn't concerned about material things like clothes or food—he focused more on leading others to Christ.

What do you care about most? Today, focus on pleasing God: live for Him, love others, and tell people about Jesus.

PURE IN HEART

The pure in heart are blessed, for they will see God. —Matthew 5:8

In this passage, Jesus says the words *pure in heart*, which mean clean thoughts and feelings.

If you struggle with being pure in heart, start by praying for God's help. Next, try to get rid of anything that is hurtful to your relationship with God (tasteless TV shows, websites, and magazines).

SETTLING QUARRELS

Leave your gift there in front of the altar. First go and be reconciled with your brother, and then come and offer your gift. —Matthew 5:24

Followers of Jesus should make it a priority to "reconcile" or settle quarrels with others. Showing God's love to friends, family, and enemies is a major theme in this chapter.

Are you currently quarreling with someone? Today, ask God for ways to end your arguments and show His love to everyone.

NO MORE WORRYING

Why do you worry about clothes? Learn how the wildflowers of the field grow: they don't labor or spin thread.
—Matthew 6:28

In today's culture, someone is judged mostly by how they look and what they have.

But God doesn't care what type of jeans you wear; He cares more about your character and relationship with Him. Today, worry less about temporary materials like your clothes and focus on the eternal God.

FOLLOW HIM

"But so you may know that the Son of Man has authority on earth to forgive sins"—then He told the paralytic, "Get up, pick up your mat, and go home."
—Matthew 9:6

In this verse, Jesus proved His authority to a group of skeptical Jewish scribes. These people were skilled at writing the Old Testament and guarding Jewish traditions.

Following Jesus is not about tradition, but it's about your personal relationship with Him. Are you following Him daily?

DEPENDING ON HIM

Don't take a traveling bag for the road, or an extra shirt, sandals, or a walking stick, for the worker is worthy of his food. —Matthew 10:10

Jesus sent the disciples to other nations so that they could spread the Good News. But He told them to leave their essential needs behind. It was better that they depended completely on God.

Do you depend completely on God? Or do you just live for Him on Sundays?

JESUS, MESSIAH, SAVIOR

"But you," He asked them, "who do you say that I am?" —Matthew 16:15

Many major religions recognize Jesus as a prophet, a wise man, and a historical figure. But who is He to you?

Today, focus on Jesus as your Savior. Live for Him during each moment of the day with what you say, how you act, and how you treat others.

LIVE LIFE TO THE FULLEST

What will it benefit a man if
he gains the whole world yet loses
his life? Or what will a man give in
exchange for his life? —Matthew 16:26

In this passage, Jesus reminded the disciples that in order to truly live, they had to make God number one in their lives.

Is there anything in your life that is taking the place of God? Today, live fully for God—make Him number one.

DON'T MISS THE POINT

"Why do you ask Me about what is good?" He said to him. "There is only One who is good. If you want to enter into life, keep the commandments."
—Matthew 19:17

In this passage, a rich young ruler asked Jesus how to earn eternal life. But the ruler missed the point.

It's impossible to earn your way into heaven. Jesus already made a way. Today, tell someone about Jesus, His sacrifice, and the free gift of salvation.

SAY WHAT?

When the disciples heard this,
they were utterly astonished
and asked, "Then who can be saved?"
—Matthew 19:25

Jesus surprised the disciples with the metaphor in verse 24. But mostly, He was making an example of the rich young ruler, a man who couldn't confess his sins or commit to following Jesus.

Today, confess your sins to God and get rid of the things that hurt your relationship with Him.

WALK THE WALK

He said to him, "Love the Lord your God with all your heart, with all your soul, and with all your mind." —Matthew 22:37

Jesus responded to the Pharisees and Sadducees' question with a quote from Deuteronomy 6:4-5. Ironically, this was something that they already knew because faithful Jews recited this several times daily.

Although they knew the answer by heart, they didn't do it. Today, don't just say you'll follow Christ, live it out!

RELIGIOUS FREEDOM

Then they will hand you over for persecution, and they will kill you. You will be hated by all nations because of My name. —Matthew 24:9

In this verse Jesus prophesied about the persecutions of His disciples.

In other parts of the world, Christians are persecuted for their beliefs. Many of them have to meet in secret churches because if they're caught, they could be imprisoned or killed. Today, be thankful for your religious freedom.

SEPTEMBER 28

GET READY

Now concerning that day and hour
no one knows—neither the angels
in heaven, nor the Son—except the
Father only. —Matthew 24:36

It's made clear that no one knows when Jesus will come back, except for God.

Although it's impossible to know, it's important to be spiritually prepared. Live each day in a way that affects heaven: love others, encourage your Christian friends, and tell people about Jesus.

THE CROSS

He saved others, but He cannot save Himself! He is the King of Israel! Let Him come down now from the cross, and we will believe in Him. —Matthew 27:42

It's important to remember what Christ endured for the sins of humanity. He didn't die just for "good Christians," but for everyone, including those who mocked Him on the cross.

Today, pray for and love someone who is hard to get along with—Christ died for that person, too.

GOD'S PROMISES

He is not here! For He has been resurrected just as He said. Come and see the place where He lay. —Matthew 28:6

When Mary Magdalene, the other Mary, and the disciples found the empty tomb, they had to remember what Jesus had prophesied and promised.

Today, take comfort in all of Jesus' promises—especially the one in Matthew 8:30: "Remember, I am with you always, to the end of the age."

I AM WHO I AM

God replied to Moses, "I AM WHO I AM. This is what you are to say to the Israelites: I AM has sent me to you."
—Exodus 3:14

When God commanded Moses to go tell Pharaoh to let the Israelites go, Moses was full of fear. This verse shows how God helped Moses to have courage. God's Words, "I AM WHO I AM," show that He has always been the same great God.

You, too, can have courage in all things because God is the same yesterday, today, and forever!

TONGUE TWISTER

Yahweh said to him, "Who made the human mouth? Who makes him mute or deaf, seeing or blind? Is it not I, Yahweh?"
—Exodus 4:11

Is there something about yourself that you wish you could change?

Moses thought that his poor speech would keep him from doing what God commanded, but God is bigger than any speech problem! God created Moses, and you, just the way He wanted you to be. Even the things that you wish were different about yourself can be used for God's glory.

275

THINGS TO REMEMBER

I am the LORD your God, who brought you out of the land of Egypt, out of the place of slavery. —Exodus 20:2

When I fell into the pool, the tarp that covered it slipped over my head. I tried to escape, but I couldn't get free. My dad pulled me out of the pool to safety. I'll never forget what he did.

In this verse, God is reminding the Israelites how He had saved them. Take time to remember all that God has done to rescue you.

AWESOME FEAR

Moses responded to the people, "Don't be afraid, for God has come to test you, so that you will fear Him and will not sin." —Exodus 20:20

Have you ever seen something so awesome that you just had to stand in awe and stare at it?

The Israelites learned that they should fear God. To fear God means you understand how big and how awesome He really is. When you realize this, it helps you draw closer to Him and move further away from sin.

I WILL OBEY

Moses came and told the people all the commands of the LORD and all the ordinances. Then all the people responded with a single voice, "We will do everything that the LORD has commanded."
—Exodus 24:3

Obedience means to submit to the commands of authority. The ultimate authority is God. God gives rules to protect you and to help you live a better life. You honor God by obeying the commands that He gives you.

When God gives you a commandment, will you say, "I will obey"?

FOLLOW THE RULES

The LORD spoke to Moses: "Go down at once! For your people you brought up from the land of Egypt have acted corruptly. They have quickly turned from the way I commanded them." —Exodus 32:7-8

"Son, I am very disappointed in you." My dad said those words to me right after I scratched his truck with my bicycle. He told me not to ride my bike in the garage, but I broke the rule. Not only did I scratch the truck, but I also hurt my father by disobeying his rules.

When you break rules, God is disappointed because you have disobeyed His commandments.

THE COST OF SIN

The following day Moses said to the people, "You have committed a grave sin. Now I will go up to the LORD; perhaps I will be able to atone for your sin."
—Exodus 32:30

Moses loved the Israelites so much that he was willing to die to pay the price for their sins. Do the actions of Moses remind you of someone else?

Moses was unable to completely cover their sin, but Jesus Christ was crucified to pay the total price of your sin. His blood has paid for your righteousness!

OCTOBER 8

GONE FISHIN'

"Follow Me," Jesus told them, "and I will make you fish for people!" —Mark 1:17

When Connor's family decided to move to Africa as missionaries, he had to give up all his friends and video games. He was upset at first, but then he realized that serving God was greater than any video game.

Following Jesus Christ might mean you have to make sacrifices. If He asked you to leave everything you own to serve Him, could you do it?

A+ TEACHER

They were astonished at His teaching
because, unlike the scribes, He was
teaching them as one having authority.
—Mark 1:22

When you're sick, who do you go see? A doctor studies for years to learn about disease and medicine and then is given the authority to diagnose your illness and prescribe medication.

Jesus has been given all authority by God. People were amazed by Jesus because His teaching and wisdom came directly from God.

HEALING HAND

When Jesus heard this, He told them, "Those who are well don't need a doctor, but the sick do need one. I didn't come to call the righteous, but sinners."
—Mark 2:17

In Jesus' day, the most disliked person in town was a tax collector. They were cruel people that often lied and stole from people. Yet Jesus chose to hang out with tax collectors and other less desirable people. Like a doctor views a sick patient, Jesus saw they needed to be healed from sin.

OCTOBER 11

JESUS, WHERE ARE YOU?

They woke Him up and said to Him, "Teacher! Don't You care that we're going to die?" —Mark 4:38

Have you ever felt like God wasn't there?

The disciples' boat was caught in a great storm, and they wondered why Jesus wasn't there to save them. Jesus had not forgotten about them, but He wanted to test their faith. When you face difficult situations and it seems like He isn't there, have faith that He is still with you.

OCTOBER 12

CARRY THE CROSS

If anyone wants to be My follower,
he must deny himself, take up his cross,
and follow Me. —Mark 8:34

Have you ever thought about what it takes to follow Christ?

Jesus taught that people would have to endure suffering and leave their possessions behind in order to follow Him. People often risk their lives to follow Him. It may not be as dangerous for you to follow Christ, but there are still sacrifices that you must make. Those things will be replaced with heavenly rewards!

DELICIOUS TEMPTATION

Stay awake and pray so that you
won't enter into temptation. The
spirit is willing, but the flesh is weak.
—Mark 14:38

Seth knew he wasn't supposed to eat the cookies, but he couldn't resist. He gave in and ate two cookies before dinner. When Seth's mom found out, she punished him for breaking the rules.

Even when you know the right thing to do, you are often tempted to do the opposite. You need to stay focused on Christ so you don't give in to each day's temptations!

A DIFFERENT KIND OF KING

Pilate asked Him, "Are You the King of the Jews?" He answered him, "You have said it." —Mark 15:2

Pilate asked Jesus this question because he didn't think Jesus fit the mold of king. Instead of riches and an army of soldiers, Jesus was standing before Pilate in chains. Even still, Jesus answered Pilate by stating that He was exactly what Pilate called Him, a King!

Jesus was a different kind of king. He was a king who came to serve the world and save the world!

A WRONG CHOICE

Pilate asked them again, "Then what do you want me to do with the One you call the King of the Jews?" Again they shouted, "Crucify Him!" —Mark 15:12-13

The mob of people were led by the chief priests, and they were convinced that Jesus was guilty. Pilate could not find any wrong Jesus had done, so he offered to free either Jesus or Barabbas, a murderer. The angry mob chose Barabbas over Jesus.

Imagine how Jesus was feeling when the people He was dying to save chose Barabbas over Him.

SHARE THE STORY

He said to them, "Go into all the world and preach the gospel to the whole creation. Whoever believes and is baptized will be saved, but whoever does not believe will be condemned."
—Mark 16:15–16

Braden prayed every day for the opportunity to share the gospel with someone at school. By the end of fifth grade, Braden had led seven of his friends to Christ. Jesus saved Braden from his sin, and Braden knew this was worth sharing!

The gospel of Jesus Christ has the power to save the lost. Will you share it?

THE MIRACULOUS BIRTH

Now listen: You will conceive and give birth to a son, and you will call His name Jesus. —Luke 1:31

Mary could not believe the announcement of the angel. She was so stunned that she had to ask, "How can this be?" Joseph and Mary were not yet married, and it was impossible for her to be pregnant. Mary was shocked because the angel told her she would give birth to the Son of God!

Remember that nothing is impossible with God!

BORN TO DIE

Today a Savior, who is Messiah the Lord, was born for you in the city of David. —Luke 2:11

The Bible says that everyone sins, and sin separates you from God. Even on your best day, you cannot reach God's standard. Jesus came to Earth to pay the price for your sin. While sin makes you an enemy of God, believing in Jesus' death and resurrection makes you a friend of God.

Thank the Lord for all He has done to save you!

DON'T GIVE IN

The Devil said to Him, "If You are the Son of God, tell this stone to become bread." But Jesus answered him, "It is written: Man must not live on bread alone." —Luke 4:3-4

Have you ever felt pressure to give in to temptation? Jesus gives you a great example in how to face temptation and not sin. When Satan tempted Him, Jesus responded by quoting Scripture. Study your Bible and store it in your heart. When you face temptation, you'll be ready to fight back with the Word of God!

OCTOBER 20

THE FULFILLMENT OF PROPHECY

He began by saying to them,
"Today as you listen, this Scripture
has been fulfilled." —Luke 4:21

The Old Testament contains hundreds of prophecies about a Messiah. Jesus fulfilled every single one of these prophecies. The One that people had been talking about and waiting on for hundreds of years was now standing right in front of them. Jesus wanted them to understand and believe that He was the Messiah.

Praise God for His awesome gift of Jesus the Messiah!

LOVE YOUR ENEMY

But I say to you who listen:
Love your enemies, do what is good
to those who hate you. —Luke 6:27

Batman had Joker, Superman had Lex Luthor, and Spiderman had Green Goblin. Everyone has enemies.

The people around Jesus hated their enemies and wanted revenge, but Jesus taught the opposite. He said that you should love them and do good to them. He wants you to show your enemies the same love that He has shown you. It may be hard, but it helps them know Jesus!

SEEING AND BELIEVING

"Go and report to John the things you have seen and heard: The blind receive their sight, the lame walk, those with skin diseases are healed, the deaf hear, the dead are raised, and the poor are told the good news." —Luke 7:22

How do you know Jesus Christ is the Messiah, the Son of God? The miraculous things that Jesus did help us to have faith in Him as King of kings. Who else could do such things?

You can believe in Jesus Christ and in all His promises because you can see that He has done great things!

SPREAD THE NEWS

"Go back to your home, and tell all that God has done for you." And off he went, proclaiming throughout the town all that Jesus had done for him. —Luke 8:39

Joshua couldn't wait for summer to end so he could go back to school. For vacation, his parents surprised him with a trip to the coolest new amusement park, and Joshua wanted to tell his friends all about it.

Jesus wants you to be like Joshua. Jesus has done so many things that are worth sharing, and He wants you to tell everyone about His goodness!

KEEP KNOCKIN'

So I say to you, keep asking, and it will be given to you. Keep searching, and you will find. Keep knocking, and the door will be opened to you. —Luke 11:9

Do you believe God listens to your prayers?

Jesus reminded His disciples that they should continue to seek God and ask for His help. Even when they did not feel like God was listening, He was. The same is true for you. Continue to ask God for His help and He will be there for you.

WHAT ARE YOU THINKING?

The Lord said to him: "Now you Pharisees clean the outside of the cup and dish, but inside you are full of greed and evil."
—Luke 11:39

I remember my pastor telling me, "The God that you worship on Sunday is the same God who is watching Monday through Saturday." He helped me to learn that God wants me to live in obedience to Him every day and in every action. This means that what I think, say, and do should always honor God even when no one else is around.

Do your thoughts and private actions honor God?

DON'T DENY IT

"I say to you, anyone who acknowledge
Me before men, the Son of Man
will also acknowledge him before the
angels of God." —Luke 12:8

On the night Jesus was arrested, Peter denied knowing
Jesus three separate times. On that scary night, Peter was
afraid of what others would think if he said he was one of
Jesus' disciples. Jesus wants you to let others know that
He is Lord. He wants you to share it in words and deeds.

Do your words and deeds show that Jesus is Lord?

REPENT! REPENT!

I'll get up, go to my father, and say to him, Father, I have sinned against heaven and in your sight. I'm no longer worthy to be called your son. Make me like one of your hired hands. —Luke 15:18–19

The son had messed up, and it was time for him to repent. Do you know what it means to repent?

Repent means that you recognize your sin and you turn to God for forgiveness. You must realize that you are not worthy because of sin, but if you repent, God, the Father, will accept you and cleanse you through the blood of His Son.

LET'S PARTY!

We had to celebrate and rejoice, because this brother of yours was dead and is alive again; he was lost and is found.
—Luke 15:32

When the son returned home, the father ran to meet him. He was so thankful that his son had come home that he just had to celebrate! God the Father is even more excited when a person accepts Jesus Christ as Savior. It's like a long lost son has come home to be with his Father!

If you are a Christian, thank God for welcoming you into His family!

CRY OUT TO JESUS

He called out, "Jesus, Son of David, have mercy on me!" —Luke 18:38

If someone is in a dangerous situation, what do they yell? "HELP! WILL ANYBODY HELP ME?"

As Jesus walked by the crowd of beggars, the blind man did not cry for help from just anybody. He cried out for help from Jesus, the only One that could heal him. When you are in need, do you cry out for the One who can help?

THE LORD'S SUPPER

In the same way He also took the cup after supper and said, "This cup is the new covenant established by My blood; it is shed for you." —Luke 22:20

This meal was the last time that Jesus would eat with His disciples because He would later be arrested and crucified. He wanted them to understand that He was about to die in order to save them eternally.

Communion, or the Lord's Supper, is a way of remembering the agony and suffering that Jesus endured for you. His blood was shed to defeat your sin and bring you salvation.'

IT'S ALL ABOUT HIM

Beginning with Moses and all the Prophets, He interpreted for them the things concerning Himself in all the Scriptures. —Luke 24:27

As J.D. listened to the Sunday school lesson about Jesus, he remembered hearing a similar story from the Old Testament. When he asked the teacher, she said, "The whole Bible points to Jesus."

On the road to Emmaus, Jesus showed two strangers how the whole Bible pointed to His death and resurrection as God's plan to save the world. Imagine learning about Jesus from Jesus!

NOVEMBER 1

THE MOST POWERFUL

Power and might are in Your hand,
and no one can stand against You.
—2 Chronicles 20:6

What do the villains of every story want? They want to rule the world. They desire to be the ones with the most power. No one will ever be as powerful as God. God holds all power in His hand. Therefore, you can trust in Him throughout all of life's circumstances. He is the ultimate power.

KNOW THE HELPER

Haven't I commanded you: be strong and courageous? Do not be afraid or discouraged, for the LORD your God is with you wherever you go. —Joshua 1:9

Is there anything you cannot do by yourself? Do you have to ask someone to help you? When you are in a tough situation, it's always good to know the right person to call. No matter what you face, you can always call on God. He's never been wrong!

YOUR PART, GOD'S PART

Be strong! We must prove ourselves
strong for our people and for the cities
of our God. May the LORD's will be done.
—2 Samuel 10:12

What does it mean to be strong? Does it mean that you are able to lift a thousand–pound weight? Does it mean that you are able to hit a grand slam and amaze all of your friends? Strong sometimes means that you are able to stand for what is right. Find your strength in God. His strength is perfect and never fails!

BE PATIENT

Wait for the LORD; be strong and
courageous. Wait for the LORD.
—Psalm 27:14

Don't you just love waiting? It is so much fun. I especially like waiting on things like summer break, for my turn to play a video game, or for my birthday! OK, you're crazy if you believe I love waiting! Waiting is hard! The Bible says you are to wait for the Lord! When you feel like you have no help, wait. When you feel lost and alone, wait. When you need courage, wait. God will answer.

BIGGER THAN YOUR TROUBLES

When the Philistine looked and
saw David, he despised him because
he was just a youth, healthy and handsome.
—1 Samuel 17:42

Imagine that you are going to fight a 9–foot giant. This giant has terrorized your friends and neighbors for days, and now you must fight him. How do you think you would feel? David found himself in this situation. He was probably nervous. But David trusted God, and God protected him. God can be trusted to help you face all your troubles.

ALL THE STRENGTH YOU NEED

The Lord GOD comes with strength,
and His power establishes His rule.
His reward is with Him, and His gifts
accompany Him. —Isaiah 40:10

Do you think you could pick up a car? There have been reports of people who lifted a car to free someone trapped underneath. In the moment of desperation, those people had strength beyond what they normally had. When you feel weak, call on God. He offers His strength to help you.

THE STRONGEST HANDS

Riches and honor come from You, and You are the ruler of everything. Power and might are in Your hand, and it is in Your hand to make great and to give strength to all. —1 Chronicles 29:12

When I was little, I always thought my dad's hands were huge. I remember how my little hand would wrap around just one of his fingers. I thought my dad was stronger than anything, and I trusted him to protect me. Now that I have a son of my own, I would do anything to protect him; however, humans are limited in power. Only God can provide total strength and protection.

MAKE THE COMMITMENT

We will do and obey everything that the LORD has commanded. —Exodus 24:7

God's commitment to you is that He will always be there for you. What is your commitment to God? In today's verse, the Israelites committed to do everything God commanded of them. Make your commitment to God to do the same. Follow His commands.

PRAISE THE POWER

May the name of God be praised forever and ever, for wisdom and power belong to Him. —Daniel 2:20

Some people think Benjamin Franklin invented electricity. But that's not true, is it? The Bible says that everything came from God! Wisdom and power belong to Him. Do you want to be wise? Get to know God better. Do you want to have power? Then have a personal relationship with God. He is the giver of all good things!

OUR RESPONSE

Give me life in accordance with Your faithful love, and I will obey the decree You have spoken. —Psalm 119:88

The most wonderful life available is one that is lived for Christ. This doesn't mean that life is going to be easy, but you have a promise from God that He will never leave you. What are you supposed to do in order to follow Jesus completely? Obey Him!

FOLLOW THE LEADER

Obey Me, and then I will be your God, and you will be My people. You must follow every way I command you so that it may go well with you. —Jeremiah 7:23

Have you ever played the game "Follow the Leader"? To be good at that game, you must do exactly what the leader does. To have all that God wants for your life, you must do exactly what He commands you to do. You will find those commands in His Word. Read it daily and follow what it says.

ONE OF A KIND

Yahweh, there is no one like You. You are great; Your name is great in power.
—Jeremiah 10:6

Look closely at your fingertips. Do you see those lines curving around? Did you know that no one else in the world has lines just like those? Your fingerprints are one of a kind. In the same way, there is no one like God. His great and mighty power sets Him apart.

THE SAME FOR YOU

All this happened so that they might keep His statutes and obey His instructions.
—Psalm 105:45

This Scripture refers to the many ways God provided for the Israelites when they left Egypt. God revealed His power by giving them food and water, by destroying their enemies, and by guiding them through the wilderness. The same God who did all of that so long ago wants to provide for all your needs today. Trust His leading and know His love.

KEEP GOING

Be strong; don't be discouraged,
for your work has a reward.
—2 Chronicles 15:7

I am sure that every time you have ever done something good you have been rewarded, right? Wrong! I am sure that you probably have done many good things that seem to have gone unnoticed. The Bible tells you not to be discouraged because you have a reward. You won't see it here on the earth; you will see it in heaven!

NOVEMBER 15

LOOK TO HIM

Wisdom and strength belong to God;
counsel and understanding are His.
—Job 12:13

Need directions? Look at a map. Question about history? Look on the Internet. Need to spell a word? Look it up in a dictionary. Whatever circumstances you face in life, you can always turn to God and His Word to find the right answers.

EXTRAORDINARY WISDOM

Look, God shows Himself exalted by His
power. Who is a teacher like Him?
—Job 36:22

I visited an electrical dam. The turbines inside the dam were huge—probably 15 feet high. Large "fins" on the turbine's side were moved by thousands of gallons of water flowing through the dam each minute. The dam was a picture of power. Just as the strength of the dam shows its power, God is exalted by His power. Learn from God and you will receive His power.

IN 3-D!

Look up and see: who created these? He brings out the starry host by number; He calls all of them by name. Because of His great power and strength, not one of them is missing. —Isaiah 40:26

One starry night in Belize, I looked up and realized that stars are actually layered. Some are closer than others, just like trees on a hillside. I could not believe the depth of the stars! It made me feel small and almost insignificant. Then I remembered that the same God who created those stars in 3-D also created me. Wow!

NO NEED TO FEAR

God has not given us a spirit of fearfulness, but one of power, love, and sound judgment. —2 Timothy 1:7

I once had to confront a really big guy. He could have pounded me into the ground and left a grease spot. But I knew that God expected me to talk to the man about things in his life that were not right. I asked God to give me the power to confront the man and relied on God's power to protect me. God did both!

POWERFUL WORDS

He made the earth by His power,
established the world by His wisdom,
and spread out the heavens by His
understanding. —Jeremiah 10:12

What is the hardest thing you have ever done? Hit a fast ball? Played an instrument? Wrote a report about nuclear physics? Knowledge is power! Before you can accomplish a difficult task, you have to know what you are doing. God made everything you see by simply saying a few words. Now that's power!

EVERYTHING YOU NEED

His divine power has given us everything required for life and godliness, through the knowledge of Him who called us by His own glory and goodness. —2 Peter 1:3

Christmas is coming. Have you made your "wish list" yet? What do you think you "need" to make your life good? Does the list include something related to knowing God? All you really need to make your life good is Jesus Christ. Make sure your list includes something that will help you know Him better.

A POWERFUL REQUEST

I will therefore do what you have asked. I will give you a wise and understanding heart, so that there has never been anyone like you before and never will be again. —1 Kings 3:12

Solomon was the wisest man who has ever lived. Most of the book of Proverbs was written by him. When he had a chance to ask God for anything he wanted, he asked for wisdom—not money, a big boat, or a sweet contract with the Yankees. He simply wanted God's wisdom in his life. If you had the chance, what would you ask God for?

THANK YOU, LORD

Give thanks to the LORD, for He is good;
His faithful love endures forever.
—1 Chronicles 16:34

Thanksgiving is more than a day. Thanksgiving should be a daily part of who you are. Are you thankful for your family? How about where you live? Can you be thankful for food and clothing? Thank God for giving you what you need. Thank the people God uses to provide these necessities for you.

FAITHFUL STRENGTH

You will lead the people You have redeemed with Your faithful love; You will guide them to Your holy dwelling with Your strength. —Exodus 15:13

When you tell a friend that you will help him, do you keep your word no matter what? Being faithful means that someone can depend on you. You do what you say you will do. There is strength in a person who sticks by his word. God's faithfulness is shown through His love. He loves you no matter what.

NOVEMBER 24

LISTEN UP

You must follow the LORD your God and fear Him. You must keep His commands and listen to His voice; you must worship Him and remain faithful to Him. —Deuteronomy 13:4

"Can you hear me now? Good." I wonder if God ever asks you that question. Without you answering with words, God knows the answer when He watches your life. If you really want to follow God, you will listen to His Word and do what it says. Through obedience, you worship Him. Can you hear God now?

THE BIG MAN'S HOUSE

Only goodness and faithful love will pursue me all the days of my life, and I will dwell in the house of the LORD as long as I live. —Psalm 23:6

If you could choose any house in the world, (to eat your Thanksgiving meal) where would it be? The White House? Grandma's house? Waffle House? The Bible talks about living in the "house of the Lord." Just think what God will give you at His house. Blessings are everywhere! There's one requirement to get in—trust Jesus as your Lord and Savior.

GUARD DUTY

Be alert, stand firm in the faith, act like a man, be strong. —1 Corinthians 16:13

Sentries are people who stand guard around a fort or camp. They must have the courage to stand when the enemy shows up—not run away. Sometimes they do it alone. Do you have the courage to stand up for the things of God? Can you be God's sentry? He will give you His power to serve if you let Him.

FORT GOD

To You, my strength, I sing
praises, because God is my stronghold—
my faithful God. —Psalm 59:17

A stronghold is a place where you can feel safe and brave. A fort allows those inside to continue living well, and it protects them from the enemy outside. God can be your stronghold when others try to influence you to do something wrong. Ask Him to be your strength when others tempt you to do bad things.

NOVEMBER 28

THANKFUL NOW

I will sacrifice to You with a voice of thanksgiving. I will fulfill what I have vowed. Salvation is from the LORD!
—Jonah 2:9

Jonah was alive in the belly of a great fish when he said these words. What would you do if you were swallowed by a great fish and lived to tell about it—thank God for saving you or complain about being in a smelly fish's gut? Avoid a smelly situation—thank God now!

HE IS . . .

You, Lord, are a compassionate and gracious God, slow to anger and rich in faithful love and truth. —Psalm 86:15

If I asked your friends to describe you, what would they say? Would they say you are nice, gracious, slow to get angry, loving, and truthful? That is exactly who God is, and He expects you to be the same. This may not be what you see in men on TV shows or in movies. But I would rather be like God than be like them. What about you?

GOD'S STRONG HAND

They are Your servants and Your people. You redeemed them by Your great power and strong hand. —Nehemiah 1:10

My grandfather's hands were strong. He was a farmer. He drove a tractor, raised cattle, moved hay bales, and ran barbed wire fences. He provided for his family with those strong hands. God provides for His family with His strong hands too. He has all power in them. If you don't know about His power, ask a Christian about how to become a part of His family.

DON'T LET GO

Hold on to instruction; don't let go.
Guard it, for it is your life.
—Proverbs 4:13

You've just gone overboard at sea. The waves are rough. The wind is whipping. Someone throws you a life preserver—your lifeline. You hold on for dear life because it is your life. Wisdom from God's Word is your lifeline. If you'll obey it, it will save you from much trouble. Hold on to it. Don't let go!

SOAR INTO BATTLE

Those who trust in the LORD will renew their strength; they will soar on wings like eagles; they will run and not grow weary; they will walk and not faint.
—Isaiah 40:31

Seventy-one years ago this week (December 7, 1941) Japan attacked Pearl Harbor. It was a devastating defeat for the U.S., but America didn't hide. Instead, the U.S. regrouped and prepared for battle.

Through the difficulties of your week, know that God can help. Let Him strengthen you today as you read His Word.

LOVE WHILE YOU WAIT

Love is patient; love is kind. Love does not envy; is not boastful; is not conceited. —1 Corinthians 13:4

"Wait a minute." Have you ever heard those words from your parents? Everyone has to wait at times—waiting to check out at the grocery store, waiting for Christmas break, waiting for your parents to help you with your homework. Patience is more than waiting. It's waiting with a good attitude. The Bible says love is willing to wait and to wait with a good attitude.

DECEMBER 4

JUST BE KIND

Be kind and compassionate to one another, forgiving one another, just as God also forgave you in Christ. —Ephesians 4:32

You probably know what it is like to be made fun of or even bullied, but God has a different plan for you. It's called kindness. That's being nice even when you may not feel like it. It's thinking of others instead of just thinking of yourself. In what way will you be kind to someone today?

ACCEPT ONE ANOTHER

Accept one another, just as the Messiah also accepted you, to the glory of God.
—Romans 15:7

"Look at his shoes." "Did you see her hair?" "I would die if my mom picked me up in that car." God judges a person by his heart, not his appearance. Making fun of someone says much more about your heart than it does about his appearance. Instead, reach out to those who aren't accepted and do what Christ did for you. He accepted you.

DECEMBER 6

READY OR NOT . . .

One will come from you to be ruler over Israel for Me. His origin is from antiquity, from eternity. —Micah 5:2

"I'm dying to see that movie." "I can't wait until Christmas."

There's something coming that's greater than the best movie and more awesome than the present. That something is actually a someone—Jesus. He came once and died for your sins. Now He's coming to rule as King. Are you ready? He's coming!

ROAD RAGE

Refrain from anger and give up your rage; do not be agitated—it can only bring harm. —Psalm 37:8

You've heard of people doing crazy things because of road rage. It's also easy to get angry at a parent, brother or sister, or someone at school. Sometimes anger gets the best of you and someone gets hurt. When anger begins brewing, try counting to 10, and tell your rage to hit the road.

STRONG HEARTS WAIT

Wait for the LORD; be courageous
and let your heart be strong.
Wait for the LORD. —Psalm 27:14

Do you like waiting? Sometimes it's really hard just to wait. You want something, and you want it right now.

Now think about God. He's never late. He's never early. God is always right on time, but it's not always in your time. That's when it takes courage. Waiting on God isn't for wimps.

GREAT NEWS!

He will be great and will be called the
Son of the Most High. —Luke 1:32

The angel told this to Mary about her coming Son, Jesus. The angel's words are called prophecy, which means "a telling of the future."

Look back at Jesus' life and the great impact He's had on the world. He is the Son of God. He came to this world as a baby to save you from your sins. Isn't that great news?

HOW TO BE HAPPY

LORD of Hosts, happy is the person who trusts in You! —Psalm 84:12

What makes you happy? Does getting what you want for Christmas make you happy?

Most things that make you happy only make you happy for a short while. Video games get old. New clothes fade. The Lord is the only One that won't fade. When you trust in Him, you know you've made the right choice. You'll be happy you did.

SWEET HOPE

Delayed hope makes the heart sick,
but fulfilled desire is a tree of life.
—Proverbs 13:12

It's overtime unless you make this shot. Hope is alive. Right at the buzzer you take a shot. The basketball rolls completely around the rim and falls into the net. Hooray!

Missing the shot and going into overtime would have been a delayed hope. Making the shot, however, was a fulfilled desire.

How sweet it is! Set your hope on God.

DECEMBER 12

WAIT FOR THE SON

Our citizenship is in heaven, from which
we also eagerly wait for a Savior, the
Lord Jesus Christ. —Philippians 3:20

If you've trusted in Christ for salvation from your sins,
you're actually a citizen of heaven even though you live
here on the earth. As a believer you're waiting for Jesus to
come back so you can be with Him in your final home. You
wait with excitement for Him to come!

SEEK AND FIND

The LORD is good to those who wait for Him, to the person who seeks Him.
—Lamentations 3:25

Hide-and-seek is a game that's been around for a long time. If you are the seeker, you look all over the place to find all the hiders.

In life, you must seek after God. Unlike your friends, He wants to be found. Yesterday, you read about waiting on God. Remember, God is just waiting on you to seek and find Him.

IMMANUEL, GOD WITH US

The virgin will become pregnant and give birth to a son, and they will name Him Immanuel, which is translated "God is with us." —Matthew 1:23

Have you ever felt alone even when other people were around? Maybe you felt alone in your pain, your sickness, your fear, or your sin.

Christmas is about God coming to you. Even though people are all around, you have a sin problem that's hopeless without Jesus being with you. When you feel alone, remember that God is with you.

NO BEGINNING?

In the beginning was the Word,
and the Word was with God,
and the Word was God. —John 1:1

You began. You had a starting point. Do you remember your birth? Maybe not, but I know that you had one.

In the verse above, Christ is the Word. He had an earthly birth, too, but He had no beginning because He is God. You will have no end in eternity, but Christ had no beginning. What a way to blow your mind at Christmas!

BORN FOR YOU

Today a Savior, who is Messiah the Lord, was born for you in the city of David. —Luke 2:11

Almost every Christmas present has one thing in common—a name tag. The presents must have tags on them to indicate to whom the gift belongs. Without name tags, no one would know which gift was for him. Jesus is the greatest Christmas gift that has ever been given, and your name is on the tag!

GOOD SHEPHERD

I am the good shepherd. I know My own sheep, and they know Me. —John 10:14

I really know my wife. I can recognize her voice instantly on the phone. I can pick out clothes that she likes. I can even predict what she will order at most restaurants. The more time we spend together, the better I know her. God is the same way. If you really want to know God, spend as much time with Him as possible.

ONE AND ONLY

For God loved the world in this way: He gave His One and Only Son, so that everyone who believes in Him will not perish but have eternal life. —John 3:16

Imagine that I cover the state of Texas with silver dollars two feet deep. I mark one of them, and instruct you to pick up the marked coin without looking. Think you could do it? According to mathematics professor Peter Stoner the above activity illustrates the odds of one person fulfilling just eight of over three hundred Messianic prophecies in the Bible. Jesus alone fulfilled them all!

ALL THIS AND MORE

A child will be born for us, a son will be given to us, and the government will be upon His shoulders. He will be named Wonderful Counselor, Mighty God, Eternal Father, Prince of Peace. —Isaiah 9:6

Sometimes it is hard to think of Jesus as a baby, doing what babies do. Jesus became human so He could pay for your sins. But Jesus is so much more than that! He is fully God. He is Savior. He is Lord. He is Messiah. He is your friend. He is so much more than you could ever expect.

THE LIGHT OF THE WORLD

As long as I am in the world, I am the light of the world. —John 9:5

Here's an experiment for you to try. Take a flashlight into a totally dark room. Now turn the flashlight on. What wins—the darkness or the light? Try it ten times. A hundred times. A million times. Light always wins. The Bible says that Jesus is the light of the world. Jesus always wins!

HIS NAME IS JESUS

Now listen: You will conceive and give birth to a son, and you will call His name Jesus. —Luke 1:31

People today generally give their children names that they like or ones that sound good. In Bible times, parents gave their children names that meant something. Jesus means "God saves." Could God have chosen a better name for Baby Jesus? I don't think so!

HE BRINGS PEACE

Glory to God in the highest heaven, and peace on earth to people He favors.
—Luke 2:14

The Bible calls Jesus the Prince of Peace because Jesus brings lasting peace. Jesus can give you three types of peace. (1) He can give you the ability to live in peace with other people. (2) He can give you internal peace to handle difficult situations in life. (3) Most importantly, Jesus can give you peace with God through His gift of forgiveness.

DECEMBER 23

TELL EVERYONE

After seeing them, they reported the message they were told about this child.
—Luke 2:17

Imagine you receive a box in the mail and open it to find one million dollars! Would you throw the box in your room and go watch television? Of course not! You would tell everyone you know. (And probably buy a few things.)

You have been given something better than one million dollars—you've been given the gift of salvation, Jesus Christ! Who do you want to tell first?

IT'S TIME!

While they were there, the time came
for her to give birth. —Luke 2:6

If you play sports or video games, you know how important timing is. God cares about timing too. The Bible says God sent Jesus to be born in Bethlehem at the perfect time.

If you have a need in your life, God will respond in His timing. You can trust Him to know your need, know what's best for you, and respond at just the right time.

MAKE ROOM FOR JESUS

Then she gave birth to her firstborn Son,
and she wrapped Him snugly in cloth and
laid Him in a feeding trough—because
there was no room for them in the inn.
—Luke 2:7

There is a lot going on today. Presents must be opened. Meals need to be prepared and eaten. Family has to be visited. Christmas day is a wonderfully exciting time! Unfortunately, many people don't make room for Jesus on His birthday. Make sure that you make room for Jesus today.

WORSHIP HIM

Where is He who has been born King of the Jews? For we saw His star in the east and have come to worship Him.
—Matthew 2:2

The word *worship* means "to express reverence and respect." When you worship God, you declare His worth to yourself and to other people. The wise men traveled quite a distance so they could declare Jesus' worth. How about you? Are you a worshipper? Worship isn't a chore you have to do on Sundays—it's a great privilege you get to do every day of the week.

GLADLY SERVE HIM

Serve the LORD with gladness;
come before Him with joyful songs.
—Psalm 100:2

Suppose I was your waiter at a restaurant. What if I brought your order, dropped it on the table, and angrily said, "Here's your food"?

You probably wouldn't tip me well, would you? Although I did what I was supposed to do (I brought your food), my attitude was terrible. Remember that your attitude matters as you serve God.

DECEMBER 28

THE RIGHT ATTITUDE

Serve the LORD with gladness;
come before Him with joyful songs.
—Psalm 100:2

You don't have to have a fabulous singing voice to come before Him with joyful songs. Still not comfortable singing in the choir? Don't worry, there are plenty of other ways you can serve God.

Volunteer to help with Vacation Bible School, collect clothes for a homeless shelter, or do chores for an elderly neighbor. The only requirement for service is to do it with gladness.

THANK HIM

I will thank the LORD with all my heart;
I will declare all Your wonderful works.
—Psalm 9:1

How do you feel when you do something nice for someone and he doesn't thank you? Those two words make a big difference because they tell you that the person recognized you did something nice for him. Take a minute and think about all God has done for you this past week. Have you thanked Him yet?

DECEMBER 30

PRAISE HIM

Praise the LORD with the lyre; make
music to Him with a ten-stringed harp.
—Psalm 33:2

I try to celebrate my children every day because they need to hear it, but also because I need to say it. I don't want to ever take my children for granted. God doesn't need your praise as much as you need to give it to Him. When you praise Him, you remember how wonderful He is! Sing to Him.

GLAD TO GO

I rejoiced with those who said to me,
"Let us go to the house of the LORD."
—Psalm 122:1

I love going to church. I enjoy seeing other people who love Jesus. I like to sing, pray, and hear the Bible explained to me. Church is fun for me, and I just don't feel right if I miss it!

Think about your attitude when you go to church. Are you rejoicing at the opportunity to go to church?